D1590048

Expression and Truth

Expression and Truth

ON THE MUSIC OF KNOWLEDGE

Lawrence Kramer

UNIVERSITY OF CALIFORNIA PRESS

BERKELEY LOS ANGELES LONDON

University of California Press, one of the most distinguished university
presses in the United States, enriches lives around the world by advancing
scholarship in the humanities, social sciences, and natural sciences. Its
activities are supported by the UC Press Foundation and by philanthropic
contributions from individuals and institutions. For more information,
visit www.ucpress.edu.

University of California Press
Berkeley and Los Angeles, California

University of California Press, Ltd.
London, England

Library of Congress Cataloging-in-Publication Data

Kramer, Lawrence, 1946-.
    Expression and truth : on the music of knowledge / Lawrence Kramer.
        p. cm.
    Includes bibliographical references and index.
    ISBN 978-0-520-27395-5 (hardcover : alk. paper)
    ISBN 978-0-520-27396-2 (pbk. : alk. paper)
    1. Music—Philosophy and aesthetics. I. Title.
    ML3800.K716 2012
    781.1′7—dc23

                                                    2012013883

Manufactured in the United States of America

21   20   19   18   17   16   15   14   13   12
10   9   8   7   6   5   4   3   2   1

In keeping with a commitment to support environmentally responsible and
sustainable printing practices, UC Press has printed this book on Rolland
Enviro100, a 100% post-consumer fiber paper that is FSC certified, deinked,
processed chlorine-free, and manufactured with renewable biogas energy. It is
acid-free and EcoLogo certified.

CONTENTS

MUSICAL EXAMPLES

ACKNOWLEDGMENTS

A few sections of Chapter 1 were published under the title "Wittgenstein's Chopin: Interdisciplinarity and 'The Music Itself,'" in *In(ter)discipline: New Languages of Criticism,* ed. Gillian Beer, Malcolm Bowie, and Beate Perrey (Oxford: Legenda, 2007). An earlier version of Chapter 2 appeared as "Speaking Melody, Melodic Speech," in *Word and Music Studies* 7, ed. Suzanne Lodato and David Urrows (Amsterdam: Rodopi, 2005). I am grateful to the publishers for permission to reprint this material.

OPENING SOLILOQUY IN LIEU OF A PREFACE

The purpose of this book is to do away with the "and" in its title.

Expression and truth are classic opposites in Western thought. Expression refers to states of mind, not states of being. If we follow J. L. Austin's procedure of classifying communicative acts by the way they are judged, then expression is faithful or unfaithful. Expressive acts may be true or false to their source, but they are neither true nor false. They are thus not what Austin calls constative, but neither are they what he calls performative, that is, utterances that succeed or fail at doing something in being uttered. The only thing expressive acts do is be what they are.

Or so we classically think—mistakenly. The classic view of expression is neither consistent with contemporary accounts of how the brain works nor able to stand up to philosophical investigation in the manner of Wittgenstein. This book seeks to perform that investigation with some help from Wittgenstein himself and from his scattered remarks on what is classically the most purely expressive of the arts and (thus) the one most removed from truth. Not by chance, that art is music.

The purpose of this book is to express the truth in expression: to perform, "happily," as Austin would say, the marriage of truth and expression and to state, truly, that what expression expresses is or may be truth.

But if so, so what? One has to ask.

The first decade of the twenty-first century has been so troubled as to revive old questions about the value of either practicing or studying the arts of expression—questions the first half of the twentieth century had posed all too acutely. The problem has been compounded since by digital technology, which renders all forms of expression both evanescent and infinitely malleable, and by the proliferation of media-manipulated modes of expression that induce a routine skepticism, even cynicism, about all expressive acts. In this context, an absorption in expression or in its study may seem not only socially irresponsible but also intellectually bankrupt. Acts of expression may still give pleasure and promise truth, but only, it may seem, on condition that we do not look too closely at either the acts or the offerings.

It is a measure of how difficult things have become that any promise to resolve these questions directly would (and perhaps should) sound both pompous and self-deceived. So I will do no more than suggest that a care for expression, for the culture of expression and the truth of expression, commits one to certain values that many may wish to preserve, even against steep odds and strong skepticism. To borrow the approach of my chief interlocutor in this text, I will seek mostly to *show* those values rather than to *say* what they are: to make my case primarily by practice, not proclamation.

The practice begins with the form of the book: a classic arch. (The image of the arch is both musical and architectural.) A pair of extended duos with Wittgenstein on expression in music frames a pair of reflections on the relationship between melody and speech, which in turn frames a central series of investigations of the enveloping terms *expression* and *truth*. This design aims to perform the book's overarching thesis by forming a truthful expression of it: a shape intimating the classical hermeneutic images of circle, spiral, and arc, and going these one better by taking the hemispheric pattern as a gateway, the frame of a threshold through which understanding may pass to and fro.

As this description suggests, *Expression and Truth* seeks not only to think truly about expression but also to think *with* it. True to its thesis, however, the book's expressive, free-flowing mode of exposition is guided by conceptual claims it hopes to make credible, one per chapter, to wit:

"Wittgenstein, Music, and the Aroma of Coffee": Expression is description.
"Speaking Melody": Expression is unvoicing.
"Expression and Truth": Expression is cognition.
"Melodic Speech": Expression is envoicing.
"Wittgenstein, Music, and the Tone of Crystal": Expression is reply.

To make this fivefold claim is to embrace a worldview in which sensing, perceiving, feeling, and understanding form neither a continuum nor a system of oppositions but a lacework movement within the medium of expression. Hence the book's subtitle: The forms of cognition become what they are by participating in the music of knowledge.

ONE

Wittgenstein, Music, and the Aroma of Coffee

EXPRESSION IS DESCRIPTION.

WHAT DOES MUSIC EXPRESS? The question is an old chestnut, and I raise it here not because I propose to answer it in some dramatic new way, but precisely because I don't. When asked concretely what a particular piece of music expresses here or there, we usually mumble out some vague, relatively stereotyped statement, from which we customarily conclude that we really can't say what music expresses. We often follow up by saying that this inexpressible expressiveness is one of the things we like best about music. In what follows, I will be defending the first half of this scenario and dismissing the second. The vague statements are all right, in much the same way that Ludwig Wittgenstein famously said that ordinary language is all right. Wittgenstein, in fact, will be my chief interlocutor here and throughout this book, a kind of duet partner, alternately playing primo and secundo.

But as for music's ineffability, for that is the issue at stake when we mumble, this notion represents an error very much like the notion that we cannot know other minds (something else that exercised Wittgenstein, who could never quite make up his own mind about the minds of others). As J. L. Austin showed in a classic essay, the possibility of knowing other minds all depends on what you mean by "know."[1] Can I form a reasonable estimate of what someone else is thinking? Of course I can. Can I think exactly the same thought amid the same sensations, as if I were myself the other person? Of course I can't. If I blurt out the comment that a certain musical passage is thoughtful, say, or poignant, my comment is obviously inadequate only if I am trying to reproduce in words the exact experience of listening to the music. But of course I'm not—unless, perhaps, I'm Proust, who had the advantage of writing at length about music that doesn't exist.

The question of musical expression may nowadays seem less urgent than it once did. Recent thinking on what music is "about" has concentrated more on its social than on its expressive force.[2] This tendency connects with the desire for a historically grounded understanding of musical meaning and it breaks with the tradition of treating feelings, the presumed substance of expression, as universals unaffected by history. My own work promotes this tendency, which I do not propose to curb or divert. Yet the question of musical expression deserves revival, because, as I hope to show before I'm through, the stakes underlying it have significant broader implications both for and beyond the way we understand music. Only if we have an adequate understanding of musical expression can we begin to understand the wider role of music in acoustic experience and auditory culture.

But let's raise the stakes: Only if we have an adequate understanding of musical expression can we begin to understand expression in general and the complex ties between the two forms of experience that give this book its title: expression and truth.

The first performance of Brahms's Clarinet Quintet was held in the grand Viennese home in which Wittgenstein grew up. Brahms was a frequent visitor at the Palais Wittgenstein, as were Gustav Mahler, Clara Schumann, and Bruno Walter. Ludwig's early years were drenched in the music prized by the Viennese classical tradition. This music was second nature to him; his love of it went without saying, perhaps too much without saying, for he rarely wrote about it. He probably kept mute because the music spoke too eloquently. The music meant too much to be talked about. Wittgenstein's attitude toward music was ascetic, almost renunciatory, in keeping with the monastic discipline that ruled his personal life. Words and pictures, his constant preoccupations, did not pose the dangers, the temptations of music: the sensuous and emotional immediacy, the power over memory, the cognitive pliability. Yet Wittgenstein could not remain altogether silent about music, either. His later writings contain a scattered handful of remarks that can help light up new aspects of music as a phenomenon. This wording, it will soon appear, is not casual. The remarks are, though; they are "about" music only indirectly. What they offer is a chance, not to rethink Wittgenstein's thoughts on the topic, but to think about music from the angle of reflection that he discovered and came to embody. It's the angle, not necessarily the thoughts issued from it, that I find most valuable.

The Wittgenstein I have in mind is not a philosopher who makes hypotheses but an aphorist who disturbs our conventional habits of thought, an observer who exposes the prismatic strangeness underlying ordinary life and takes the results at face value. This is the Wittgenstein who asks in all seriousness why his right hand can't give his left hand money (*Philosophical Investigations* 1958, 94; hereafter, *PI*) and ponders whether a stone in pain could be said to have a soul (*PI*, 97).[3] He is a thinker who affirms the authority of experience by refusing to submit experience to higher authority. He is a writer who sharpens description where others call for explanation. And he is in some ways not entirely himself—not, at any rate, the therapeutic figure who dispels false problems by appealing to the grammar of our language games but an incurably fascinated figure who yields to the countervailing enchantments of life in all its perplexity to voice a grammar of intimate estrangement, the grammar of no grammar. He disenchants metaphysics, yes, but he does it to re-enchant the world.

I don't know whether I have read or invented this Wittgenstein, whose original is such an iconic and much-appropriated figure that the question is moot: Despite the fact that Wittgenstein really existed, we have to invent him.[4] But invention is also a musical form, and one that is not a bad metaphor for Wittgenstein's practice, which typically picks up a theme and subjects it to a series of variations, embellishments, inversions, and counterpoints. At times, it even seems that music is Wittgenstein's intuitive model of intelligible utterance. He treats it as an irreducible combination of mystery and clarity to which language should learn to lay claim: "Speech without thought and not without thought should be compared to playing a piece of music without thought and not without thought" (*PI*, 109).[5]

Which is not to say, all too hastily, that we should prefer the route of thought. The two routes are alternatives, not contraries; each leads to places we might want to go. Speaking without thought may become the discovery of what has not yet been thought, what is hidden from thought or forbidden it; playing a piece of music without thought (as he often does, Wittgenstein is thinking of the piano, the center of musical life in the culture of his youth) may be the best way to tap a fine-tuned expressive instinct, to enter into the spirit of a mood, attitude, or feeling that thought might retard or subvert. We can always do our thinking afterward.

As now: for questions come crowding in here. Let's say that when we play or speak with thought, we articulate our thought; when we play or speak without thought, we express ourselves. This distinction is provisional: a first move. The opposition of articulation and expression begins to collapse almost as soon as it's made, but the timing and manner of its collapse are revealing. Ask about this in the manner of Wittgenstein: When you're playing a piece of music, say a Chopin prelude (Wittgenstein will speak of "a reflective Chopin"), how do you know you're not thinking? Don't you have to think about that? Isn't the way you play a form of thinking? And if you exclaim afterward, "I don't know how I did that!" or something of the sort, is that speaking with thought or without? Doesn't the *that!* presuppose a certain conception, the very thing about your playing that satisfied you, that seemed true to you or to the piece?

Questions like these can be multiplied endlessly. It's a matter of fact, of common experience, that we take some communicative actions as articulations and some as expressions, but there's always an element of decision in doing so, and perhaps an element of pretense or fantasy. Articulation is always also performative; it has an expressive dimension. Just so, expression is always also articulate; it entails substantive claims. Austin said of speech acts that they are all both constative and performative. It's easy to say that nowadays; saying so has become a common speech act in its own right. The hard thing is to keep the idea in mind and let it affect one's practice.

As with this: There is a habitual asymmetry between articulation and expression that we should both think about and play on. This asymmetry is important, not just because of what it says (articulates? expresses?) about language and music but because it deeply affects the way we experience the world.

We usually grant authority to what we think independently of what we feel about our thought, at least insofar as we try to honor the truth. Ideally, when we say what we think, we say what we think is true. But we don't grant the same authority to what we feel (intuit, imagine, fantasize), which we regard as unlinked from the truth precisely insofar as we merely express our feeling. We require that the truth come at the feeling from the outside, or else we accept that it can't and we value or devalue the feeling on its own terms, which are inevitably the lesser terms.

This is a mistake. Our expressive acts are as much (and as little) capable of describing the world truthfully as our articulations. Like articulations, expressions also contribute to what they describe. Not that expressive acts fabricate: If they succeed, what they do is make something apparent. In making something apparent, they also make its interpretation possible. To say so is to grant these acts a power of descriptive realism denied to them by the blind elevation of articulation over expression. Unlike the initial, merely provisional opposition of articulation and expression, this either/or is for real. To grant or deny the power of descriptive realism is to enrich or impoverish our experience.

Experience is the key: the locale where both concepts and feelings are lived out, lived by, lived through. The asymmetry—articulation over expression—has a further dimension that comes closer to the metaphysical bias that continually devalues experience. (By this I want also to say: continually devalues reason, in the most ideal post-Enlightenment sense. But this cannot be said quite yet, except indirectly, via expression.) Both speaking and playing a piece of music are acoustic events. Their relationship to the truth is mediated by the ear, not the eye; they work by matching a fluctuating contour of pitches and rhythms, the substrate of voice and bodily activity, with ideas or feelings. Good matches make for strong meanings. Good matches convey power and authority from the speaker or performer to the listener. But some go further.

What is said can also be written. Articulation both demands and provides the possibility of transmission; in principle, the articulate is articulate permanently as long as it can find a storage medium. What is expressed cannot be written. Expression consumes itself in the moment. It can be documented and recorded but not repeated; information storage is a record of its loss.

Like the original distinction between articulation and expression, this distinction between storage and loss begins to collapse as soon as it is made. But the exact character of its collapse is a source of great significance. Rearticulation demands reexpression. To say something over is to play it a new way, apply it to new circumstances, activate the performative element always latent in it. Anything that can be revisited yields to this dynamic, which is as active as it is inexorable. Articulations happen neither once nor many times but something in between. Revisiting is revising. And although expressive acts do, and can, happen only once, recorded expressions can be reanimated by grasping their connection to what has been articulated through them. Even acts of unrecorded expression may linger and perhaps intensify in the storage medium of cultural or personal memory. The "only once" of expression has no fixed duration.

It is experience that tells, in every sense of the phrase. Experience thrives on neither the visual nor the acoustic, the articulate nor the expressive, the permanent nor the temporary, but only on the constant spillage or collapse of each into the other. The traditional subordination of the fluid to the more rigid terms only leaves us high and dry. Thought holds the heights in imperial solitude and demands conformity to the letter of its law; experience becomes arid and solaces itself with what it takes for mirages and oases.

This sundering is the condition that Wittgenstein memorably described as being held captive by a picture (*PI*, 48). As his own practice shows (he never quite said it), the choice to step out of the frame leads to a rearticulation of the world. The choice makes expression and truth stranger, stronger, and richer in possibility than they could be otherwise. When we make this choice we resolve on that. Yet the choice really resolves nothing: In choosing we merely set ourselves a task that has to be renewed constantly because it is so easy to forget in practice the basic principle that Wittgenstein expressed in the saying "Words are deeds," together with its corollary, which he left out, that doing speaks.[6]

So, in the spirit of the Wittgenstein I have conjured here, and what I think of as the descriptive realism that impels his incessant thought experiments and makes itself known in quasi-musical clusters of short paragraphs with the tight weave of prose poetry, I want to consider the experience of musical expression, an experience that is both musical and, just because it is musical, more than musical. In the spirit of descriptive realism, any understanding won from this effort should be expressly regarded, not as a thesis offered in the transparency of thought, but as a venture made amid the opacities of language. We are already caught in the meshes of the word, tangled in musical metaphors just as Wittgenstein's "speech without thought" (gedankenloses Sprechen), is caught between meaning careless and unreflective speech, and there is, happily, no way out.

"Soulful expression in music," says Wittgenstein, "—it can't be recognized by rules."[7] How can it be recognized, then? How do we know soulfulness when we hear it? Wittgenstein says we don't have to know how we know: "If a theme, a phrase, suddenly says something to you, you don't need to be able to explain. It's suddenly just *this* gesture that's accessible to you." You just suddenly get it.

This is not to say that such getting is not also a giving; to recognize a meaning is always in part to endow with meaning. But all this, as Wittgenstein might say, is implied in the grammar of "getting it." The metaphor of music suddenly speaking in a way that sparks this *eureka!* experience helps explain the lack of any need for explanation. "The speech of music. Don't forget that a poem, although constructed in the language of communication, is not used in the language-game of communication" (Z, 28).[8] Like the words of a poem, a musical phrase can "go through and through us" (uns durch und durch gehen), a sensation framed in part by the way we "let our thoughts roam this way and that in the familiar surroundings of the words" (Z, 28).[9] The enhanced understanding does not correspond to the familiarity, but to the roaming. The familiarity relieves us of the need to explain (I don't have to explain how I understand this sentence), while the roaming takes the familiar outside itself, expands into the not yet known.

Of course, to have this experience at all I must know how to listen or play, just as I must know the language of the poem. If, need aside, an explanation of soulful expression were still required, its basis would be acculturation: "Someone who is brought up in a certain culture—then reacts to music in such-and-such a way, to him you can teach the use of the words 'expressive playing.'" Such a person would know how to imagine an expressive performance of the music, or be able to describe the expressivity of a particular performance, or have the capacity to reflect on the expressive content in an informed way. For such a person—and any listener must be such a person—the music has no identity, hardly has an existence, apart from the possibility of its being played or heard expressively. Expression, which is to some degree coextensive with the "language game" of music, requires extension, otherness, going beyond (what we construe as) the notes.

Music is mute. It does not speak and it cannot be made to speak. (So we're told, anyway; perhaps making it speak is not impossible, only frowned upon). This concept is a historical consequence of the rise to preeminence of instrumental concert music in post-Enlightenment Europe. In a sense, the concept is a false universal, since most of the world's music was and is vocal music. But once the idea of a speechless music, music as speechlessness incarnate, is historically established, once the possibility has been discovered and elaborated, music acquires the power to reduce any and all sung words to mere phonetic substance, even if the listener still understands them, which is by no means always the case. Language dissolves into the music itself the moment there is such a thing. The old canard that music expresses what words cannot finds no serious resistance from vocal music; rather the reverse. To give music back its lost voice is to deny and defy the regime of music's muteness, the regime that strikes it dumb.

Music has the force of verbal expression or description without the substance. It is like a seemingly grammatical sentence that says nothing: "Colorless green ideas sleep furiously" is the standard example. Like a figure on a staircase drawn by Escher, you can never get to where it leads. Why do we take this strange thing so much for granted? And what would happen if we didn't?

Wittgenstein wondered, too:

> Couldn't we think that a man who has never known music and who comes to us and hears someone playing a reflective Chopin, that he would be convinced that this is a language and we just want to keep the meaning secret from him?
>
> In verbal language there is a strongly musical element. (A sigh, the intonation of a question, of an announcement, of longing, all the numberless gestures [*Gesten*] of intonation.) (*Z*, 29)

Wittgenstein's tone-deaf guest doesn't know how to recognize music, and just for that reason he perceives something true about it that is normally glossed over. The music is hiding something; it has a hard edge. Those who know music have learned how to treat this hiding not as a lack but a gift. For them—"us"—music reveals and conceals its meaning at the same time, so that we get an inkling of the meaning in the moment it eludes us, which is every moment. And knowing music, we know that the little semantic vortex that results is supposed to leave us giddy with pleasure.

Wittgenstein links this experience to the sphere of inflection rather than articulation: Music flows in and out of the continuously fluctuating tonality of speech, here figured as a strongly physical as well as a strongly musical medium, one in which, or *that* in which, knowledge (sought in a question, found in an announcement) and desire (even the unlimited desire of Romantic longing) blend into a continuum.

But there is more to the music than this, more *in* it than this. Wittgenstein does not speak here about just any music, but about music by Chopin, and more particularly about reflective music by Chopin—even such music "as" Chopin, as it were a piece of him, not just of "his." In Wittgenstein's elliptical phrasing the music is "a reflective Chopin" (nachdenklichen Chopin). (The phrasing plays us, plays on us, precisely because we know what it means without having to think about it.) Unlike the tone-deaf guest, those of us who know music hear Chopin when someone plays Chopin. We hear the music's gestures of intonation—a question, an announcement, longing—knit together by a process of reflection that lies transparently open before us. "Chopin" is the name we give to this process in its singularity, and by giving the process this name we make possible a full and open hearing that would otherwise elude us. This "Chopin" is a fabrication, but its consequence is the music's reality.

Wittgenstein's presentation of "someone" playing a reflective Chopin is remarkably close to Jane Welsh Carlyle's impression of Chopin himself doing so in 1843: "[Chopin's music] is not a specimen of art offered to the general admiration. . . . It is rather a reflection of part of his soul, and a fragment of his life lavished on those who have ears to hear and a heart to understand."[10] Wittgenstein's tone-deaf guest hears only the specimen of art, which, oddly enough, lacks the signature of the artist: Chopin without "Chopin." Because the tone-deaf guest does not know music by ear or by heart, because he does not, in Wittgensteinian terms, know how to do anything with or say anything about what he hears, he cannot make the leap to the fragment of life lavished on him. So he responds to the music's Cheshire-cat purr—its message with a vanishing meaning like a smile with a vanishing face—with resentment. And in a way he is right to do so. Chopin's reflective music, the paradigm of musical reflectiveness in general, really is a kind of secret language, a paradigm for the secretiveness of language in general. But the secret kept by language is always an open secret, the action of which, disclosed without disclosure, is itself a form of meaning.

Chopin's role in the history of feeling thus blends with Wittgenstein's inquiry into the lived character of language. The tone of a reflective Chopin even blends with the feeling of that inquiry's own lived character, its own musical gesture of intonation, much as it might have done in the Wittgenstein mansion in fin de siècle Vienna where someone would so often come and hear someone playing.

What does it mean to perceive an object "as" something? Wittgenstein kept coming back to this question. It was initially a matter of simple perception, famously illustrated by the duck-rabbit, a line drawing that could be seen as either animal but not both at once. But from simple perception the question branched out to embrace fiction, metaphor, and what might broadly be called perceived conception. What goes on, Wittgenstein wanted to know, when I perceive a chair as a fort? What about when I perceive a smile now as an invitation, now as a threat, now as true, now as false? What happens when I hear a melody as a lament?

These questions were not looking for explanations of subjective phenomena; a leading theme of Wittgenstein's later writings is the futility of just that. ("All *explanation* must go," he wrote [Alle *Erklärung* muss fort, *PI,* 47], "and only description take its place.") The questions were meant to elicit descriptions of human actions and the forms of life embodied by them. How, exactly, do I act when I perceive an object "as" something? How does the perception act on me? What do I want from the object and it from me? What happens?

Wittgenstein responds by talking about changes in "aspect." When I see a smile as a threat rather than a greeting, a different aspect of the smile comes to the fore. One aspect is switched on, so to speak, while another aspect switches off. The change of circumstance or interpretation is realized by the "lighting up"—*Aufleuchtung*—of an aspect. This new aspect is not discernible in itself. We see by the new aspect but do not see it. Nor does it correspond to a physical or material change, or even to a change in appearance. "But what is different?" Wittgenstein asks, "My impression? My point of view?—Can I say? I *describe* the change like a perception quite as if the object had changed before my eyes" (*PI,* 195). There is nothing above or beyond that description, which is neither literal nor metaphorical but merely truthful. "The expression of a change of aspect is the expression of a *new* perception, simultaneous with the expression of an unchanged perception" (*PI,* 196). I see nothing new in the object; I just see the object in a new way. Yet there is nothing paradoxical about this experience. It is the most familiar, most natural thing in the world. If the experience baffles us, that is only because we allow ourselves to forget that its remarkable qualities are part of the fabric of our ordinary experience and need to be neither explained nor demystified, but only investigated.

When does that investigation lead us to music? What aspect of music does it end by lighting up?

Wittgenstein habitually identifies perceiving-as with seeing-as, as if unconsciously swayed by the general tendency in Western thought to equate knowledge with vision. Yet he does observe, even if he does not quite acknowledge, a difference between seeing-as and hearing-as. His examples suggest that seeing-as is usually instantaneous; that it usually jumps abruptly from seeing an object now this way, now that; and that what we see is usually seen as unambiguously present. His definition of aspect change embraces all these tendencies: "I contemplate a face, suddenly I notice its similarity to another. I *see* that it hasn't changed; and still see it otherwise" (*PI,* 193). Elsewhere, still more forcefully: "We don't see facial contortions and now *infer* (like a doctor making a diagnosis) joy, sadness, boredom. We describe a face immediately as sad, radiantly happy, bored, even when we aren't able to give another description of the facial features" (*Z,* 41). Breaks in this visual immediacy have a threatening quality, as if they endangered the texture of phenomenality itself. The examples given are few and disconcerting: a familiar object made unrecognizable by unfamiliar lighting or position, the inability to recognize someone after a lapse or years or in a crowd (*PI,* 197).

Hearing-as is altogether different. Wittgenstein's examples, most of them involving music, suggest that hearing-as usually involves a deferral; that it usually marks a transition from *not* hearing-as, that is, from nonsense to sense rather than from sense to sense; and that what is heard is only ambiguously present in—but this is my term, not his—the music's sounding presence. (In, as we used to say, "the music itself." If we still express ourselves this way, it is because this sort of "itself" is a necessary fiction, or at least one that has proved to be unavoidable. In truth there "is" no music itself, no bounded self to music, except as a moment in our passage from one other to another.[11])

Let's take these things up one at a time:

1. For Wittgenstein, hearing-as in music is modeled on performing-as; musical expression is to the ear what expressive performance is to the hands (the implied medium is usually the piano). This process takes time. In principle hearing-as involves sorting through alternatives until the right one presents itself:

> I have a theme repeated to me and each time played in a slower tempo. Finally I say "*Now* it's right," or "*Now* at last it's a march" or "*Now* at last it's a dance." (*PI,* 206)

The right aspect lights up in an abruptly enhanced present moment: the italicized *Now.* The italics mark an exclamation that is also an echo of the sound that breaks through like a light. The Now of seeing-as is typically much less marked, less sharply distinguished from the time before it.

2. The time before hearing-as is expressively indefinite. Before one hears the repeated theme as a march or a dance, one doesn't hear it as much of

anything. Wittgenstein imagines someone deficient in seeing-as whom he calls aspect-blind; we might suggest that a period of being aspect-deaf is built in to the experience of music.

Insofar as hearing-as moves from the sound of some mute pre-intelligible substance to the music of an aspect, as if the aspect were lit up in the auditory dark, hearing-as is the Ur-form of perceiving-as. Before it is heard as something, music embodies the "it" of the phrase "it makes sense" apart from any sense it might make. This separation, however, is not absolute, which is why, luckily for us, music is never "absolute," either. Although, as Wittgenstein says, one can hear a musical phrase apart from the special feeling or sentiment (*Empfindung*) that it gives us, what one hears in that case is not yet music. One can't hear the music itself until one hears it as something else. Only from the perspective of that "as" can one even speak of the music itself. This is not a purely conceptual formulation, but a description of what the experience is like. Where visual uncertainty brings anxiety, the uncertainty of the music itself brings pleasure. Or, more precisely, the uncertainty of the music itself *repeats* the pleasure that *follows* it when we hear the music as this or that. The music itself is always that which will have become the music-as.

Conversely, the music-as is that which may have been, and may yet become, the "it" of the music itself. When, as sometimes happens, I hear music *as* something right off, the possibility of losing the *-as* remains as part of the horizon of my listening. The music may even seek to install that loss the better to induce the pleasure of music in between the *it-* and the *-as*, and the richer to make the *-as* when it comes to me and I to it. This primordial play of pronouns has a meaning and a music of its own.

3. The content of musical expression is neither in the music nor outside of it. Unlike seeing-as, hearing-as does not give its outcome a *place*. If I see a face as sad, I know how to locate the sadness in the person whose face it is. If I hear a melody as sad, the sadness "belongs" only to the melody. "Sad" is simply what the melody is. Yet there is no lack here, not even an absence; although we have no term for it, the nonlocality of musical expression is a positive quality. It becomes even more so when one goes beyond blunt terms like *sad* and enters the arena of modern musical hermeneutics, where one might hear a melody, or whatever, as, say, nostalgic for the utopia of a form that its own construction renders ideologically remote.

The *-as* of music goes far beyond Wittgenstein's generic categories to incorporate frames of reference that are exact and elaborate—to steal a phrase from Wittgenstein himself that will concern us in chapter 5. Music dissolves meaning in order to precipitate it. But in doing so acoustic music is exemplary of the epistemic flux that forms the music of knowledge. The comforts of seeing-as are necessary but temporary. The cardinal features of hearing-as--the wavering of recognition, the acuteness of the *Now!*, the relinquishing of place—are the marks of an encompassing resonance.

Wittgenstein plays out the fluidity of musical expression through the ambiguities of the loaded word *Empfindung*, which can mean "sensation," "feeling," "perception," and "sentiment," and in the case of the last carries long-standing connotations of refinement and emotional quickness:

> Just think of the expression: "I heard a lamenting [klagende] melody"! And now the question: "Did he *hear* the lament?"
> And if I answer: "No, he didn't hear it; he only got a feeling of it" [er empfindet es]—what does that accomplish? One certainly can't pretend even once to name a sense organ for this "feeling" [Man kann ja nicht einmal ein Sinnesorgan dieser "Empfindung" angeben].
> Some might now reply: "Of course I hear it!"—Some: "I don't really *hear* it."
> But conceptual distinctions can be established. (*PI,* 209)

The last statement notwithstanding, no conceptual distinctions are established, either here or elsewhere. On the contrary, it is the futility of such distinctions, rendered here in the Janus-faced identity of hearing and not hearing, that gives us the feeling, *die Empfindung,* of hearing-as.

Music in the realm of Western listening must be described before it can be interpreted: In that respect music is like everything else. But there is also a respect in which music must be described even before it can be heard. It can be heard intelligibly only "under a description" in the philosophical sense of the term.[12] (A "description," in this special sense, is the answer to the question "What are you doing?" The question, of course, does not actually have to be put into words, but it does have to be understood. It makes a difference whether I am snapping my fingers to call a dog, express impatience, or insult someone.) Apart from such descriptions, whether potential or actual, there is no "work" of music, no music itself, though there may be musical sounds in abundance. Music must always be reconstituted to be constituted in the first place. The case is suggestively similar with dreams, which have to be put into textual form not just to be interpreted but also to be remembered. Like unvoiced dreams, the music itself can only show itself and vanish.

The very things that are supposed to be the objects of description can suddenly turn out to be the means of description. Here is Wittgenstein noticing how metaphors of understanding pervade the common forms of musical description: "If I say, e.g., it's as if a conclusion were being drawn here [in this music], or as if here something were confirmed, or as if *this* were an answer to something earlier,—my understanding just so presupposes a familiarity with conclusions, confirmations, answers" (Z, 31).[13] Strip away the "as if" clauses and the metaphors appear in their musical guises, forms that disguise their own metaphorical character: cadence, key, counterpoint. The statements that Wittgenstein invokes are speech acts that not only report but also enact understanding, and their relationship to the objects they describe is completely reversible. That is, I could perfectly well understand a passage of prose by saying, "It's as if a cadence came here, or as if a new key had been found."

Perhaps this is why Wittgenstein, reworking his figures of understanding, elsewhere treats understanding speech and understanding melody as essentially the same activity:

> Understanding a sentence in speech is more closely related to understanding a theme in music than one might suspect. What I mean, though, is this: that the understanding of a spoken sentence lies nearer than one thinks to what one ordinarily terms the understanding of a musical theme. Why should dynamics and tempo move in just *this* line? One would like to say: "Because I know what it all means." But what does it mean? I wouldn't know how to say. To "explain" I could only compare it with something else that had the same rhythm (I mean the same line). (One says: "Don't you see, it's as if a conclusion were being drawn," or "That's like a parenthesis," etc.) (*PI*, 143)[14]

The meaning comes from anywhere but the sentence or the theme. It comes from a rhythm, a line of action traced in time, that becomes fully perceptible only when I make, that is, perform, a certain kind of description, a persuasive comparison. The sentence and the theme mean precisely nothing. In fact, these supposedly solid and familiar entities may not even make sense as phenomena. How exactly does one experience the sentence apart from its use, a theme apart from its expression? Why do we even want to or think we ought to?

Wittgenstein points to one answer in a suggestive passage that draws an implicit parallel between the sound of music and something supposedly more humble, but no less hard to grasp in its very definiteness:

> Describe the aroma of coffee!—Why doesn't it work? Are the words for it lacking? And *for what* are they lacking?—But how do we get the idea that such a description must after all be possible? Have you ever felt the lack of such a description? Have you tried to describe the aroma and not succeeded?
> (I would like to say: "These notes say something glorious, but I don't know what. These notes are a powerful gesture, but I can't set something explanatory by their side." A grave nod. James: "The words are lacking." Why don't we supply them, then? What would have to be the case for us to do it?)
> (*PI*, 159)[15]

The difference between the music and the coffee lies in that somewhat satirical grave nod. The questions about the coffee are again rhetorical: Because we don't have a standard language game for describing the aroma of coffee, merely one for remarking on it, few of us have ever felt the lack of such a description. But there *is* a language game for describing music, or rather a cluster of such games, and they do sometimes fail us. We might want to say, in a Wittgensteinian spirit, that there is an ordinary language of musical description that usually suffices us: "It's as if a conclusion were being drawn," "*That* way of playing it is expressive, *seelenvoll*." We talk about things like powerful (tremendous, shattering) climaxes in contexts where the rudimentary or clichéd character of the language is unimportant; the speech acts do their work. But there is also a language game for music that depends on its own inadequacy, a game of reversal whose speech acts *undo* their work: "These notes say something glorious but I don't know what." But why play? Why take away in one breath what you give in another? Why pretend that descriptions of music are an order of magnitude less effective than descriptions of anything else—say the aroma of coffee?

Although he often wrote without fetters ("Schubert is irreligious and melancholy"), Wittgenstein, like many others, fretted over the inchoate "experience-content" (Erlebnisinhalt) of music.[16] Music forms around an experience-content that it neither conceals nor declares. This positive indefiniteness is music's mode of utterance, and even Wittgenstein, the great advocate of concepts without boundaries, stumbled over it. So did Gustav Mahler, whose music Wittgenstein could not hear "with understanding" and thus thought "worthless."[17] Mahler stumbled eloquently: "I know for myself that as long as my experience (Erlebnis) can be summed up in words, I would certainly make no music about it. My need to express myself [mich . . . auszusprechen] musically-symphonically begins only there where the *dark* sensations [dunkeln Empfindungen] reign."[18]

Vladimir Jankélévitch built an entire musical aesthetic around this game. He would write highly evocative descriptions that ended where Mahler began, on the threshold of "the *dark* sensations." For Jankélévitch, music reveals the "meaning of meaning" by concealing meaning.[19] But to say so brushes aside the obvious questions: *Meaning of what meaning? What kinds of meaning?* and at the same time sweeps the multiplicity of possible answers into a single container: *the* meaning of "meaning." Both sides of the "of" become hollow. The result is a hermetic affirmation of a situation that left Wittgenstein impatient: "But when I hear a melody with understanding, doesn't something special go on in me—that doesn't go on when I hear it without understanding? And *what?* -- No answer comes; or what occurs to me is vapid" (*Z*, 29).

Music regarded as ineffable is the byproduct of the language game embodied by Mahler's "*dark*," its intonation and double meaning included. The speech acts involved leave us speechless, and we value the momentary lack, perhaps, because precisely this kind of failure of words is a traditional trope for the experience of the sublime, the revelatory, the transcendental. We act this trope out whenever, accosted by perceptual excess, we sigh or catch our breath, murmur or cry out—when we call on the auditory to make our wonder audible. We pass from the babble of cliché to the cry of exclamation that runs the gamut from the sacred to the profane. There is, we might want to say, a language game for the performance of the transcendental in which music takes the lead.

This game, moreover, is not only played in, or with, the present. Historical acts of musical understanding often look misguided or irresponsibly "subjective" to later interpreters, but reveal their rationality when placed in historical context. What were once successful ordinary descriptions evolve into failed extraordinary ones. Most of Wittgenstein's own descriptions seem old-fashioned at the distance of a half century. Even something as simple, as seemingly neutral, as calling a passage "glorious" can sound a little embarrassing in the ironic, pastiche-laden postmodern world. Most descriptions, most interpretations of any kind, can expect at best to be destined to this kind of obsolescence. But the descriptions do not on that account become invalid or illegitimate, nor do they stand exposed as mere semantic barnacles encrusting the pristine surface of the music itself. The process of understanding evoked by Wittgenstein involves a sort of situational body heat based on the urgencies of time, place, and circumstance. When the performative urgency cools, meaning hardens and shrinks, as if turning to stone. But the urgency can be brought back to life in a vivid enough retrospect.

Consider the constant nineteenth-century habit of assigning emotions expressed in music to the person of the composer, especially if the emotions are painful. The animating context is the double one of the era's inability to conceive of subjectivity apart from an actual subject, except in the uncanny form of the automaton, and the idealization of suffering as a sign of spiritual distinction. Hence Heine's remarks on Meyerbeer: "How is it that an artist . . . destined far more than any mortal artist for good fortune—how is it that he has nonetheless felt that enormous pain that sobs and sighs out to us from his music? For what he has not felt himself, the musician cannot express so powerfully, so shockingly. . . . The artist is that child of whom the fairy tale relates that its tears become pure pearls."[20] For Heine, pain cannot be expressed powerfully unless it is sincere, so it is safe to assume its sincerity on the basis of its power. The same expressive power and power of expression is the magical means by which the pain is embodied and revalued, by which tears become pearls. We know, all appearances to the contrary, that Meyerbeer must have suffered enormously because the music itself says so by the sobbing and sighing that suddenly speaks to Heine. What makes such past commentary as his viable is not only our ability to recover the historical moment of its viability, but also its real relationship to the music, which it understands—correctly—as courting description as a person might court love or understanding.

During his tour of England and Scotland in 1848, deeply depressed and correctly convinced that his own death was near, Chopin repeatedly played "a funeral march"—presumably the famous march from his op. 35

Sonata—when asked to perform in private.[21] Evidently he needed to hear something in this music, needed to hear it as something, perhaps as the survival of his sensibility after his body's death, perhaps as the tragic dignity of his passing, or perhaps as something darker and more tortured, the self-consuming substance of his depression. On one occasion, whatever he heard became appallingly clear, though only to him. Or so we're told: A reputable collector of Chopiniana reported the incident on the basis of an original source, a letter, supposed to have been lost.[22] But the story makes sense even if it is only a fiction about Chopin, which in a way it remains even if the event really happened.

This is what Chopin is said to have said: "I had played the Allegro and the Scherzo [of the B-flat Minor Sonata] more or less correctly. I was about to attack the March when suddenly I saw arising from the body of my piano those cursed creatures which had appeared to me one lugubrious night [in Majorca]. I had to leave for one instant to pull myself together, after which I continued without saying anything."[23] Chopin had been desperately ill in Majorca some ten years before and described the small "cell" where he slept as "shaped like a tall coffin."[24] The "cursed creatures" he encountered again as revenants seem to be harbingers of death, bearers of portent like the banshee or incubus. As they arise, they identify the body of the piano with Chopin's own body. It is "my piano," he says, and whose body could be more identified with the piano than his? Whereupon the creatures turn these bodies into vessels of death, the coffins, graves, crypts of a gothic churchyard. Displacing the music but also expressing its spirit, the cursed creatures intrude a terrified silence on the music that is doubly mortal for Chopin, the silence of his death as both man and musician, the silence, the horror, of an ear that can no longer hear, a hand that can no longer play.

Chopin hears the music as what these cursed creatures embody; the creatures are tropes, figures, allegories, gargoyles, for what the music becomes—not expresses, but becomes—in this hearing. But the shape of this becoming, in the form of the creatures, is separated from the music, whose onset the creatures block. On this one occasion, Chopin hesitated to release the power of hearing-as; he acted to protect the music from becoming the advancing march of his death. But in so doing, he lost something he did not yet know he had: the power of the music to protect him from the very creatures whose silence it reversed. To hear the music as his death was bad; not to hear it as his death was worse. Just to hear the music itself, without the death it harbored, was to hear nothing, a sound more void than silence. So Chopin withdrew a moment to pull himself together, to compose himself, so to speak. And this in turn enabled him to consign his own voice to the music, both in the immediate present and the posthumous future, so that he could keep silent about what had happened to him—so that he could silence the silence.

Or did he just tell himself not to be ridiculous, to forget about things that go bump in the night and just go back and play the music "more or less correctly"? If so, was he coming to his senses or denying them? Would it even have been possible for *him*, above all, to hear *this* music, above all, without hearing it as something burdened with mortality? At what point in this whole fantastic scene could Chopin have gotten (his) death off his hands?

Musical expression resists description. So we're told. It's commonplace to say that no verbal formula, no matter how rich, can fully represent what even the simplest piece of music expresses. The statement is not wrong, but the wrong conclusion—that the truly musical value remains unaccounted for, a secret that can only be lost to the imperial force of language—is consistently drawn from it. Music presents no resistance to language that is not already fully formed in language itself.

The immediate object of any interpretation is always a description of the proposed object rather than that object itself. The description thus has the difficult task of opening up interpretive possibilities without predetermining their outcome. No merely "objective" description, in the usual sense of the term—empirical, impartial, conceptually closed—can do this. A description that claims to stick just to the facts, and postulates its own adequacy in this fidelity, is completely unable to formulate meaning and instead actually distances and neutralizes its object. Only a description that grants its own approximateness, its own figurative, conjectural, constructive character, can hope to energize the object and bring it rewardingly close.

From a hermeneutic standpoint—and this can't be said too strongly or too often—it is precisely the semantic gap between interpretation and the object interpreted that is constitutive of meaning. That gap must be preserved, not closed, to speak effectively of the artwork, or for that matter of any event or circumstance with a meaning in question. The act of description required by the object's inability to speak for itself is an encounter with otherness in the most positive sense of the term. The risk of exceeding the knowledge protocols available to one as a historical subject—that is, the risk of being "subjective" in the sense of eccentric, too "personal"—is a necessary condition of effective description.

What would happen if we examined the commonplace about words and music according to the Wittgensteinian mandate: If we didn't take for granted, but regarded as something remarkable, the fact that no interpretation can fully represent a piece of music?

Imagine an interpretation that does tell us something we can hear in a piece, something that we want to hear, even as we always, necessarily, hear more. Let it be something simple, say that a piece by Chopin is reflective; it sounds like thinking, like a meditation or reverie. To the extent that the description "applies," to the extent that we accept it as a rough template through which to listen, the music simply becomes an embodied thinking, a reverie in the mind without the mind. We hear the music differently than we would otherwise—if, for example, we heard it not in terms of "thoughtful" but of "thoughtless" expression. Any work of music can be heard under any number of descriptions of this kind, and offer in return any number of different aspects. Music does this with a distinct sensuous immediacy and a seductive, "touching" intimacy that set it apart, and perhaps are responsible for the idea that musical expression can be grasped only in musical experience. But this is an illusion, however pleasing it may be. The aspect-logic of music, its pliability under informal, relatively nonspecific description, is anything but unique. Virtually everything that figures in our world beyond the level of sheer sensation, everything that goes into the making of what Wittgenstein called a form of life, behaves in exactly the same way. We may listen to our music as we drink our coffee, but the expressiveness of the one is not that same as the aroma of the other.

During Chopin's lifetime and for many years after his death in 1849, both he and his music were consistently described in terms suggesting disembodiment: They were ethereal, angelic, elfin, sylphlike, fairy forms.[25] They seemed to occupy a border zone between spirit and matter to which they alone had access. Implicit in this way of hearing Chopin is a recognition that music outside the sphere of his exceptionality, music in general, is weighty with a bodily being that it may embrace or seek to surmount but can never forget for long. Another aspect of the Chopin legend, the emphasis on his frailty and sickliness, allied to a morbid sensibility, may bespeak the burden of that memory. But the burden creeps in even where Chopin's body is at its most diaphanous:

> As frail as he was in body, was he delicate in style; a bit more, and he evaporated into the impalpable and imperceptible. . . . Only the divine pen that described the fantastic retinue of the dream fairy [Queen Mab, that is, Shakespeare] could analyze the complicated, infinite, and yet light-as-lace tangle of that phrase charged with notes, in the folds of which the composer always enveloped his ideas.[26]

What is most striking about this obituary tribute is its slippage from the vaporous and impalpable to the soft materiality of tangled cloth, of lace and other "stuffs" as such fabrics are called, charged, weighed down with acoustic matter in the rich, delicate yet sensuous folds. We no longer listen to Chopin under this description. It would embarrass us to do so. But we could.

What do we speak about when we speak about music? Statements about expressive content are usually referred to the subjectivity of the speaker; statements about form or structure are usually referred to the music. The assumptions that underlie this distinction are effectively the same as those underlying the model of language associated with logical positivism in the early twentieth century. This is the very model or "picture" of the relation between language and truth said by the later Wittgenstein to have held his younger self captive (*PI*, 48). The distinction is based on the ease with which we can verify the statements, and thus on the degree of certainty with which they can be credited. The expressive statements have the inferior status here; they are regarded as mere "pseudo-statements" about the music itself. The analytic statements are stronger stuff, or so the old picture would have us believe.[27]

Analytic statements may not give us the whole truth about music, which after all has an expressive content even if we can't specify it. But reports of formal characteristics are thought to give us the only truth available. In short, we may or may not agree with Wagner's claim that the first theme of Beethoven's *Coriolan* Overture expresses the hero's untamable force and arrogance, but we cannot deny that this theme is recapitulated at the subdominant.[28]

The positivist view of language is, of course, long gone, but as applied to music it has great staying power; it can still seem like simple common sense when not stated too baldly. What disappears at the level of principle returns at the level of practice. Most musical analysts will now readily admit (or at least admit when pressed) that statements about form or structure do not represent music positivistically, "as it really is." Instead such statements constitute descriptions relative to an implicit or explicit, formal or informal theory of musical articulation. The statements are true to the theory more than to the music itself. Yet the positivist ideal is continually reinstated by the assumption that statements about form or structure are more fundamental and more reliable than statements about expressive content. Analytical descriptions are still widely taken to have priority over hermeneutic ones. Analytic statements are taken as propositions that specify musical realities to which all hermeneutic descriptions have to make both reference and deference. The recapitulation at the subdominant still trumps the force and arrogance.

But there is no warrant for this priority. It is no more than the effect of a long-standing language game that enwraps little truths—this theme is recapitulated at the subdominant—with the transcendental aura of a big truth. If both analytic and hermeneutic statements are forms of description, the priority of one over the other is a matter of practice, not principle. For E. T. A. Hoffmann in 1813, priority went to expression, not to structure, and it did so in a lopsided way: "That composer alone has mastered the secrets of harmony who knows how, by their means, to work upon the human soul; for him, numerical proportions, which to the dull grammarian are no more than cold, lifeless problems in arithmetic, become magical compounds from which to conjure up a magic world."[29] The underlying metaphor here is alchemy, not logic; the metaphor treats structure not as the basis of expression but as the base metal from which expression is sublimated.

In short, it is *no more true* that the first theme of the *Coriolan* Overture recapitulates at the subdominant than that the theme represents the hero's force and arrogance. It is not *made* more true by the fact—if it is a fact—that explicit criteria are available for recognizing a subdominant but not for recognizing force and arrogance. In Wittgensteinian terms, such criteria are part of the language game for specifying harmony, but not of the language game for specifying expressiveness. The usual "positivizing" suppositions about such criteria, moreover, do not always hold up. Explicit criteria are not always reliable or unambiguous, nor is their absence always a source of dubious judgments. It is easy to imagine an analytic argument to the effect that the recapitulation of the *Coriolan* Overture is not "really" subdominant, but it is hard to imagine not hearing *something like* force and arrogance in the overture's first theme. Either the force and arrogance are as much a part of the music as the subdominant recapitulation, or the music itself lies somewhere outside either one.

Both sides of this either/or are perhaps equally right. On one hand, the music can be understood as the product rather than the object of musical descriptions. The act of description specifies a form of perception and in so doing conjures up the "picture" of an object to be perceived. This is not to say, of course, that all descriptions are equally good. They manifestly are not. The first theme of the *Coriolan* Overture is not pastoral and its recapitulation is not at the flat supertonic. The fact that we can only hear under a description does not mean that we can hear under just any description. But what matters about a particular description is not its type, but its effect, its power to animate listening with pleasure and knowledge. For most listeners, the statements that do this best are more expressive than formal. Musical aesthetics has for too long labored under the illusion that such descriptions are the least faithful to the music itself.

On the other hand, no description, no matter how effective, has an exclusive claim on the music itself. For again, it is the very act of listening under a description that tends to produce an intuition of the music itself, a music that soars beyond the grasp of every particular description but not beyond the apprehension of the listener. This, too, is an illusion, but only in the affirmative sense of a trick of the senses—*trompe d'oeill, trompe d'oreille*—a perception one can't help having despite one's conceptual knowledge that it is false.

Wittgenstein's writings constantly try to mimic the rise and fall of intonation. His texts are full of exclamations, questions, and imaginary utterances, and especially of italicized words and phrases. They are full, too, of deictics, "shifters," of *this* and *that* turned into instruments of thought. This is both philosophy by intonation and the philosophy *of* intonation. It is thinking with the musicality of thought.

Is this just a matter of sensibility or style, or is there some deeper reason?

There is. If writing is, as it is traditionally understood to be, a sign for speech, then italics and a few punctuation marks—a small but hardy band of visual signals—are signs for intonation. What the italics and so on signify is a change of voice, which readers must somehow hear even if, as is most likely, the reading is done silently. This is quite literally true with Wittgenstein in particular, since he tended to dictate his typescripts. The words that would be printed in italics would have to be underlined, so that the typist would perform the equivalent of the vocal emphasis by going over the same spaces twice, once with letters and once with the repeated underline. The speech emphasis would translate immediately as the repeated keystroke.

This intonational script of written language is often suppressed in "good" writing. This point of style, enforced by a small army of teachers and editors, is the symptom of a bias that it also helps produce. It positions language on the side of reason rather than mere feeling; it objectifies the linguistic act regardless of the act's content. It silences the vocal dimension of language on behalf of a generic voice of authority.

It is precisely this voice that Wittgenstein sets out to dismantle. His power to do so no doubt stems primarily from his critical undoing of its pretensions, but this work of critique would be incomplete, perhaps even impossible, without the language that voices it, the language that philosophizes expressively about the philosophy of expression. It is no accident that this mode of thinking repeatedly leads Wittgenstein to imagine situations in which whatever happens, be it trivial or momentous, is dependent on the expressiveness of speech. No expression, no event.

From which we conclude what?

First, that the effect of expression is as much cognitive as it is affective. Expression may sometimes follow or supplement the understanding of an utterance or situation, but it is sometimes the precondition for understanding either or both. Cognition without expression makes as little sense as expression without cognition.

Second, expression is essentially an auditory phenomenon. It occurs on the threshold between voice and speech. What appears as expression in any other register or medium is a lived metaphor for a change of intonation. Language, even spoken language, is not so much expressive in itself as enunciated in the medium of expression. If, as Austin would claim after Wittgenstein, the meaning of any utterance is bound to its context, and so may change completely as the context changes, then the expressive line of the utterance, its intonational movement, is the first element in any and every context. Expression is, as we might "express" it, the context of context, the lived, embodied principle of contextuality.

Musical expression becomes particularly significant in this connection. It does so in part because the "music" of an utterance is something between a synonym and a metaphor for its expressiveness. In part, though, and perhaps the larger part, music, in expressing one thing or another, also always expresses the condition of possibility for expression itself. Music is expression in its most concentrated form. We might almost say that the phrase "musical expression" is a tautology. Expression is just *that*, and it is both remarkable and perfectly ordinary that we always know what *that* is, even if we have some trouble saying so. When we understand what music expresses, we dissolve it into our comprehension. Musical meaning diffuses itself through us like milk through coffee.

To know music in any genuine sense, we must become adept at moving between expression and the unexpressed. Although Wittgenstein is not explicit on the topic, it would appear that he simply identifies expression with the possibility of a certain type of inexact but irresistible verbalization. Music is paradigmatic of the expressive because expressiveness occurs when we sense, and in particular when we hear, something being said to us without being able to say what. We may hear this something in the tones of music or in a tone of voice; we may read it between the lines in the tone of a text or in the tone of our own voices when we are moved to speak. In response, we clumsily say whatever comes to our lips; we make a description and reject it in the same breath. The content of the statement matters less than the existence of this language game, which informs our sense of a significant world or, better, informs our world with an *atmosphere*—Wittgenstein's word—of significance and evokes the sense of sense itself.

But Wittgenstein's own language may be taken to imply exactly the opposite. This atmosphere is not the shroud of expression but its medium. Our descriptions are not the end and substance of expression, but the means by which we elicit certain aspects from the music and in that very act endow the music with a consistency that stands behind and supports the face, the aspect, that we present to it. This consistency is not a metaphysical phantom, but a concrete product of our listening practice, and one that manifests itself to us in a sensuous material form.

The movement between expression and the unexpressed corresponds to the sinuous flow (think here of the serpentine shape identified in the eighteenth century as the line of beauty) of conceptual transformation, of symbolic substitution, and, in the classic Lacanian formulation, of desire. This flow is perhaps best conceived as a temporal equivalent to the space of hybridity described by Homi Bhabha as the core condition of twenty-first-century cultural formation. The description draws out the implications of a liminal symbolic space that is also an everyday object: "The hither and thither of a stairwell, the temporal passage that it allows, prevents identities at either end of it from settling into primordial polarities. This interstitial passage between fixed identifications opens up the possibility of a cultural hybridity that entertains difference without an assumed or imposed hierarchy."[30] The stairwell winds between levels, identities, disciplines; motion along it, and under it, behind stairs, affords a continuous shifting of perspective and orientation.

As a model for thought, the stairwell involves a continuous transformation of descriptive terms into metaphors, speech acts, texts that interpret, texts to be interpreted. In following that model, I have sought (and will seek) to emulate Wittgenstein without imitating him; to use his oddly angled observations as a means of reconceiving musical expression in ways that help both clarify and dissolve its mundane force; to draw on the procedures of defamiliarization, lapidary writing, and thought experiment to inform and sustain a mode of inquiry based on the work and pleasure of thinking between, enjoying between, and living between. For it is there, in the interspaces and the interludes, that we discover the space of our own animation, the space of the lifelikeness of life and its knowledges.

The cognitive form of the result, referred to earlier under the name of "descriptive realism," is the ultimate issue here, especially, but not exclusively, as that result is reached—perhaps reached best—by the proximate issue, the experience of music. At stake is an entry in the ongoing debate about realist versus constructivist modes of understanding that is perhaps the dominant trope of knowledge in the academic world today and the primary source of the (in)famous conflict of the faculties. More broadly, the stakes are those of struggles over the status and sources of truth that seem increasingly to pervade social and political life on a global scale, but with a complexity that could only remain penumbral here. What I have sought to propose, via music, via Wittgenstein, is a small piece of an unaccomplished whole, a Wittgensteinian language game, if you like. The speech acts involved have the aim, not of producing realistic descriptions in the familiar empirical sense, but of recognizing how descriptions help produce realities that are, nonetheless, independent of every particular description. Such realities are fully capable of serving as points of reference against which the interpretive claims of the descriptions can also be understood as what Jürgen Habermas calls validity claims.[31] One such reality is what we call musical expression.

Descriptive realism is the understanding that description is what gives us access to reality, that meaning arises where and when this happens, and that meaning is not something affixed to a prior reality but something that suffuses and reshapes a reality of which it is a part. The world as we inhabit it has "intonations" like those that Wittgenstein focuses on in speech, and one mode of response to those intonations—which we partly hear, partly over-hear, partly project from ourselves—is to sing, whistle, hum, play, improvise, compose. Musical expression answers the expression of a world, in much the same way that, according to Wittgenstein, to understand a sentence is to understand a form of life. One way to symbolize or paraphrase the under-standing that results would be to say that meaning is the music of reality.

What would music be if we could hear it (not just hear the sounds, but hear the music) without hearing it *as* anything? Would we even recognize it as music, and, even if we did, would we enjoy it or be repelled by it? This question is more like a question about understanding a sentence in language than one might suspect. Is it possible for me to hear a sentence in a language I understand without understanding the sentence? If so, what would I hear? One answer would be babble, meaningless noise, made doubly senseless by the latent presence of a sense I must actively suppress because, in truth, I under-stand it at the same time as I do not. I would hear the debris of an expression that could not take place. What I would *not* hear is the sentence, which has no existence apart from my hearing it *as* a sentence. The sentence is not an acoustic substance to which a meaning is affixed: no sense, no sentence.

Music follows this logic in reverse, and it does so repeatedly, in a percep-tual process that is also a cultural ritual. As Wittgenstein's account suggests, hearing-as in music is often deferred, even if only a little: No meaning, no music, but the former must often catch up with the latter and we sometimes take pleasure in drawing out the delay. Before long, however, perception demands an aspect. We hear music *as* something, as expressing something, because there is no other way to keep hearing it. Music is not the rabbit hole down which meaning falls and disappears. Music is not a mysterious substrate to which meaning is, always falsely or inadequately, affixed. Music is a sensuous form in which meaning is both inchoate and immanent. It is something that will always have been something more; it is the threshold of that becoming other on which it is also pleasant to linger. One way to define music is precisely as meaning in its material form.

"I think," writes Wittgenstein, "of quite a short phrase, only two bars. You say 'There's really a lot in there!' But it is only so to speak an optical illusion if you think that what is in there goes on while you listen. ('It all depends *who* says it.') (Only in the stream of thought and life do words have meaning.) (*Z*, 31).[32] So the phrase has meaning only in relation to a stream that flows through and away from the two bars (they might just as well be two words) that contain such a lot. The stream is what the phrase contains without being able to hold; the flow of thought and life is what carries the passing illusion that one can hear the phrase itself.

The perception that something is "in there," that there's really a lot in there, is the imaginary form of a readiness to make educated guesses about how such a phrase might be treated, what might be done with it, how one might describe what comes of it. It all depends on who is speaking, which for Wittgenstein means on what kind of language games the speaker is ready and able to play. Such games, such speakers, fall into a finite repertoire, even a fairly small one. (I am always conscious, these days, of how small the "classical music" game—my game—has become, which, of course, only increases my determination to play it.) After observing that soulful expression in music can't be recognized by rules, Wittgenstein wonders aloud, "Why can't we imagine it might be, by other beings?" Perhaps the best answer is that any such beings would be tone-deaf by definition. Only guessing games will work here. The guesses called for do not actually need to be made. The unacted potential of making them is part of what keeps us absorbed when we listen. But the moment a guess is ventured, however offhandedly—a moment that always comes—the moment you detect expressive performance or the lack of it, the moment you represent what you've heard, even just as glorious, the music lights up. It gives us the light we hear by.

NOTES

1. J. L. Austin, "Other Minds" (1946), in *Philosophical Papers,* 3rd ed., ed. J. O. Urmson and G. J. Warnock (New York, Oxford University Press, 1990), 76–116.

2. Rather than cite the usual suspects, suffice it here to mention the recent surge of musicological interest in the writings of Theodor Adorno, for whom the social force of musical form was a first principle. To take one example among many, a recent translation of Adorno's short, experimental essay "Schubert" prompted a series of responses by a half dozen contemporary scholars, collected, along with the translation, in *19*[th]*-Century Music* 29 (Summer, 2005): 3–63.

3. Ludwig Wittgenstein, *Philosophical Investigations,* 2nd ed., trans. G. E. M. Anscombe (New York: Macmillan, 1958). The text is bilingual; the translations here and throughout are mine.

4. To each his own Wittgenstein, I suppose, as to each (including Wittgenstein) his own Freud. But "my" Wittgenstein bears a family resemblance to Stanley Cavell's, the evolution of which spans Cavell's whole career. For a sampling, see Cavell's *The Claim of Reason: Wittgenstein, Skepticism, Morality and Tragedy* (1979; repr. New York: Oxford University Press, 1999); "The Uncanniness of the Ordinary" in *In Quest of the Ordinary: Lines of Skepticism and Romanticism* (Chicago: University of Chicago Press, 1988), 153–78; and, for Cavell's own account of how "his" Wittgenstein came to be, "Epilogue: The *Investigations*' Everyday Aesthetic of Itself," in *The Cavell Reader*, ed. Stephen Mulhall (Oxford: Blackwell, 1996), 369–89.

5. "Gedenkenloses und nicht gedankenloses Sprechen ist zu vergleichen dem gedankenlosen und nicht gedankenlosen Spielen eines Musikstücks."

6. Ludwig Wittgenstein, *Philosophical Grammar*, ed. Rush Rhees, trans. Anthony Kenny (Berkeley: University of California Press, 1974), 182. The statement appears as "Words are also deeds" (*Worte sind auch Täten*) in *PI*, 146.

7. Ludwig Wittgenstein, *Zettel*, ed. G. E. M. Anscombe and G. H. von Wright, trans. G. E. M. Anscombe (Berkeley: University of California Press, 1970), 28. This volume (hereafter *Z*) is a collection of writings from the post-1945 period of the *Philosophical Investigations;* the translation, here and throughout, is again mine. The original reads: "Der seelenvolle Ausdruck in der Musik,—er ist doch nicht nach Regeln zu erkennen."

8. "Das Sprechen der Musik. Vergiss nicht, dass ein Gedicht, wenn auch in der Sprache der Mitteilung abgefasst, nicht im Sprachspiel der Mitteilung verwendet wird."

9. ". . . unsere Gedanken dorthin und dahin in die wohlbekannte Umgebung der Worte schweifen lassen."

10. Quoted in Arthur Hedley, *Chopin* (London: Dent, 1963), 323.

11. For demonstrations, see Michael Klein, *Intertextuality in Western Art Music* (Bloomington, IN: Indiana University Press, 2005); Lawrence Kramer, *Interpreting Music* (Berkeley: University of California Press, 2010); and Susan McClary, *Conventional Wisdom: The Content of Musical Form* (Berkeley: University of California Press, 2000).

12. See G. E. M. Anscombe, *Intention* (Oxford: Blackwell, 1959), 37–44; and Ian Hacking, *Rewriting the Soul: Multiple Personality and the Sciences of Memory* (Princeton: Princeton University Press, 1995), 234–35.

13. "Wenn ich z.B. sage: Es ist, als ob hier ein Schluss gezogen würde oder, als ob hier etwas bekräftigt würde oder, als ob dies eine Antwort auf das Frühere wäre,—so setzt mein Verständnis eben die Vertrautheit mit Schlüssen, Bekräftigen, Antworten voraus."

14. "Das Verstehen eines Satzes der Sprache ist dem Verstehen eines Themas in der Musik viel verwandtner, als man etwa glaubt. Ich meine es aber so: dass das Verstehen des sprachlichen Satzes näher, als man denkt, dem liegt, was man gewöhnlich Verstehen des musikalichen Themas nennt. Warum sollen sich Stärke und Tempo gerade in dieser Linie bewegen. Man möchte sagen: 'Weill ich weiss, was das alles heisst.' Aber was heisst es? Ich wüsste es nicht zu sagen. Zur 'Erklärung' könnte ich

es mit etwas anderem vergleichen, was denselben Rhythmus (ich meine, dieselbe Linie) hat. (Man sagt: 'Siehst du nicht, das ist, als würde eine Schlussfolgerung gezogen' oder: 'Das ist gleichsam eine Parenthese,' etc.")

15. "Beschrieb das Aroma des Kaffees!—Warum geht es nicht? Fehlen uns die Worte? Und *wofür* fehlen sie uns?—Woher aber der Gedanke, es müsse doch so eine Beschriebung möglch sein? Ist dir so eine Beschreibung je abgegangen? Hast du versucht, das Aroma zi beschrieben, und es ist nicht gelungen?

(Ich möchte sagen 'Diese Töne sagen etwas herrliches, aber ich weiss nicht was.' Diese Töne sind eine starke Geste, aber ich kann ihr nichts erklärendes an die Seite stellen. Eine tief ernstes Kopfnicken. James: 'Es fehlen unds die Worte.' Warum führen wir sie dann nicht ein? Was müsste der Fall sein, damit wir es könnten?")

16. Wittgenstein, *Culture and Value*, ed. G. H. von Wright in collaboration with Heikki Nyman, trans. Peter Winch (Chicago: University of Chicago Press, 1994), 47 (Schubert); 70 (Erlebenisinhalt).

17. *Culture and Value*, 67. Wittgenstein added that it obviously "took *a set of vary rare talents* to make this bad music."

18. Mahler to Max Marschalk, 16 March 1896; quoted in Siglind Bruhn, *Voicing the Ineffable: Musical Representations of Religious Experience* (Hillsdale, NY: Pendragon Press, 2002), 52, n. 12; my translation.

19. Vladimir Jankélévich, *Music and the Ineffable*, trans. Carolyn Abbate (Princeton: Princeton University Press, 2003), 46. For a critique of ineffability with respect to music, and its revival in recent thinking, see my "Oracular Musicology; or, Faking the Ineffable," in *Archiv für Musikwissenschaft* 69 (2012).

20. *Poetry and Prose of Heinrich Heine*, trans. and ed. Frederick Ewen (New York: Citadel Press, 1948), 753.

21. Jeremy Siepmann, *Chopin: The Reluctant Romantic* (Boston: Northeastern University Press, 1995), 211.

22. See Jeffrey Kallberg, "Chopin's March, Chopin's Death," *19th-Century Music* 25 (2001), 22–23.

23. Quoted in Siepmann, 217.

24. Letter of December 28, 1838; quoted in Siepmann, 140.

25. For a survey of this imagery and an interpretation with reference to concepts of sexual ambivalence and androgyny, see Jeffrey Kallberg, *Chopin at the Boundaries: Sex, History, and the Musical Genre* (Cambridge, MA: Harvard University Press, 1996), 62–86.

26. See Kallberg, 66.

27. For a fuller critique, see "Analysis" in Kramer, *Interpreting Music*, 144–61.

28. For a full account, see Kramer, "The Strange Case of Beethoven's *Coriolan*," *Musical Quarterly* 79 (1995), 256–80, repr. in Lawrence Kramer, *Critical Musicology and the Responsibility of Response: Selected Essays* (Aldershot: Ashgate, 2006), 69–94.

29. E. T. A. Hoffmann, "Beethoven's Instrumental Music," trans. Oliver Strunk, in Strunk, ed., *Source Readings in Music History: The Romantic Era* (New York: Norton, 1965), 39. For a detailed account of Hoffmann's musical aesthetics (and

their surprising relationship to his work as a jurist), see Keith Chapin, "Sublime Experience and Ironic Action: E.T. A. Hoffmann and the Use of Music for Life," in *Musical Meaning and Human Values*, ed. Keith Chapin and Lawrence Kramer (New York: Fordham University Press, 2009), 32–58.

30. Homi K. Bhabha, *The Locations of Culture* (New York: Routledge, 1994), 4; the stairwell is part of an installation by the artist and writer Renée Green.

31. Jürgen Habermas, "What is Universal Pragmatics?" in Habermas, *Communication and the Evolution of Society*, trans. Thomas McCarthy (London: Heineman, 1979), 1–3, 28–31.

32. "Ich denke an eine ganz kurze von nur zwei Takten. Du sagst: 'Was liegt nicht alles in ihr!' Aber es ist nur sozusagen eine optische Täuschung, wenn du denkst, beim Höre gehe vor, was in ihr liegt. ('Es kommt drauf an, wer's sagt.') (Nur in dem Fluss der Gedenken und des Lebens haben die Worte Bedeutung.)" Note Wittgenstein's elision of the word *Phrase,* which enacts the illusoriness that his paragraph describes.

Speaking Melody

EXPRESSION IS UNVOICING.

A cry is not a description. But there are transitions.
And the words "I am afraid" can be closer or further from a cry.
—WITTGENSTEIN, *Philosophical Investigations*

THE MOST SUCCESSFUL SONGS are those that are not always sung.
They are the songs that have so absorbed their own words that their melody
alone can substitute for the original union of words and music. They are the
songs that have so permeated their now expendable words that the words
can scarcely be spoken or written or even thought without our hearing the
music in the mind's ear. Such songs act culturally via a double process of
condensation, a term worth taking in its Freudian as well as its common
sense: Words plus music condense to music alone, and the music condenses to
a short phrase or two, to which a similarly condensed verbal phrase attaches
without being uttered.

These synoptic phrases occur where expression as the echo of a truth claim
gives way to expression as the performance of a truth. Played or extracted
without voice, circulated widely in everyday life and the media, the synoptic
phrase rises toward the status of a primary expressive form like a gesture, a
nonverbal sound, a facial expression. The members of this expressive genre
have the feel of something elemental, though in fact they are historically
bounded, and temporarily stabilized groups of them form a repertoire that in
its use creates the qualitative sense of a period's living present that Raymond
Williams identified as the structure of feeling.[1]

Melody that lacks its words yet still conveys what the words say—
speaking melody, melody that speaks when it is not sung—is so basic to such
repertoires that for all intents and purposes it *is* elemental. It is so not just
because of the power of music to suffuse itself into almost any occasion, but

more radically because speaking melody embodies the independent claim of expression as such to an immediate truth that can be grasped reflectively only through descriptions that follow (on) the expressive instance. In no other phenomenon is the relationship of expression and truth closer or more perceptible.

The descriptions that report on this relationship come about not because we supply the absent words when we hear the melody but because the absence of the words invites us to detach them from their original context so that they act as tropes, with their original meanings, both explicit and implicit, extended, supplemented, transformed, even negated.

This process, too, is historically bounded and therefore historically revealing. One reason why Beethoven's graphic portrayal of Napoleonic battle—no, not the *Eroica;* it was *Wellington's Victory*—made a big splash in its day but fell into disrepute later (though it has never fallen wholly out of the repertoire) is that the work makes programmatic use of "God Save the King" and "Malbrouck," the latter a tune better known as "The Bear Came Over the Mountain" or "For He's a Jolly Good Fellow." It's hard for us today to hear these tunes outside their aura of official patriotism on one hand and tub-thumping silliness on the other. But in 1812, when Beethoven wrote the piece, the tunes would not have sounded that way at all. They would have been, and were, heard as true expressions of national character, untouched by irony or comedy. Like the famous onion of Ibsen's Peer Gynt (for whom Grieg wrote music that has helped define what we mean by radiant sunrises and sinister underworlds), these speaking melodies seem to form around a pungent but intangible essence that gets stronger when its outer layers, the verbal integuments, are peeled away—and then disappears.

Speaking melody is a device basic to accompanied song, to musical theater, and even to instrumental music, but there has been virtually no theorizing about it. We hear speaking melody a lot but have not heard a lot about it. We need to hear more.

The relationship between music and the spoken word is usually conceived in terms of actual sound: A segment of music supports, enhances, subverts, or obscures a speech act. But with speaking melody, only the music is actual; the relationship of the music to the words is all virtual. The result is a transformation that would no doubt be heard as remarkable were it not so familiar.

When a musical phrase associated with certain words is used expressively without the words being either uttered or sung, the bare music carries the force of utterance. Speaking melody is songlike but not song, not speech but still speechlike; there is nothing else quite like it. The melody, precisely, does not sing; it speaks, and what it says is definite and understood, as if a phantom voice (there and not there, like a phantom limb) had uttered the substance of the words without their sound.

What kind of substance is this? How does it sound? What does it feel like? What does it mean?

One basis for answering these questions is Slavoj Žižek's effort to theorize the relationship of words and of pictures to what he, following Jacques Lacan, calls the Real, the unsymbolizable substrate of reality in the usual sense of the term. Voice figures importantly in this model but music does not, a defect I hope to rectify. A second basis is the anatomy of speaking melody itself, a kind of triple counterpoint involving the melody per se, the words virtually enunciated by it, and the "melody" of intonation—the palette of timbres, breath sounds, pitch contours, vibrations, inflections, and so on—available to speech as material support and to music as an object of imitation.

Starting from the last, these elements form a continuum passing from inarticulate vocal substance through the partial articulateness of speech united with melody in song to the full articulateness of spoken language. The flow of intonation, however, pulses energetically through even the most articulate speech, and so the continuum runs on. It ends with the absorption and sublimation of speech in speaking melody, an outcome that also, and paradoxically, closes a circle by reuniting speech with the acoustic substance, the expressive materiality, of the intonational matrix. This encounter at the limit entails the recognition of a material or musical excess, sometimes slight, sometimes more. My theorization will accordingly dwell on concepts of excess, surplus, and remainder. But before we arrive at that point, the phenomenon of speaking melody requires some further description and some further specification of its historical horizon.

Speaking melody ought to make no sense. It is a surplus somehow produced by subtraction. Yet it makes abundant sense, seemingly without effort. Verbal and melodic utterances share the fundamental semantic trait of iterability, the capacity to be repeated sensibly in an indefinite variety of different contexts independent of origin and custom.[2] But the act of joining words to music seems to create the potential for the music to assume the iterability of the words in the words' absence. It may be impossible to say just why that potential is or is not realized; we know it by its effects, by the panoply of speaking melodies that form, so to speak, the melosphere of any particular structure of feeling. We can, however, point to a certain typical imbalance in the conjunction of words and music that manifests itself in the production of speaking melody. The words seem to saturate the music, which cannot escape their having been uttered, but in the process the words are dissolved, assimilated, consumed. This process, to be sure, occurs within certain limitations. Most of the words involved are simply effaced. Those that persist in speaking melody tend to be simple—just a phrase or two, sometimes memorable, sometimes not—and they tend to have come at the beginnings of melodies or in refrains, the segments of music most likely to be recalled or repeated with the words unvocalized. The remarkable thing is how articulate those unvocalized segments can be.

Such musicalized speech in the absence of words conveys the verbal utterance as an intentional object rather than as an object of perception. We know the words but do not hear them; they bypass the senses that the music addresses. The language is distilled to a kind of essence, a term meant here in the double sense of a core of spirit or meaning and of a volatile liquid known by the penetrating aroma it leaves behind when it has seemed to vanish. Speaking melody channels the semantic flux of music into a definite but transient form, something not just nameable but named. In so doing, it both reveals and protects against a dread of meaninglessness that lurks at the fringes of much musical experience. Speaking melody highlights both the charismatic value of the musical aphorism—the mystique of the Proustian "little phrase"—and the vacuity potentially created by its repetition.

From one point of view, widely held in the eighteenth century, speaking melody is best understood as an explicit or reflexive form of the basic condition of melody itself. For Jean-Jacques Rousseau, melody is precisely an imitation of speech; its expressive contour mimics the intonational flow of expressive verbal utterance: "By imitating the inflections of the voice, melody expresses plaints, cries of suffering or joy, threats, moans; all the vocal signs of the passions fall within its province. It imitates the accents of [various] languages as well as the idiomatic expressions commonly associated in each one of them with given movements of the soul. . . . This is where musical imitation acquires its power, and song its hold on sensitive hearts."[3]

At best, of course, this claim takes a historically limited repertoire of melodies as a universal norm, but its obsolescence as a proposition does not exhaust its force. The underlying notion that melody distills expressive speech to its essence has great durability. And it is not always tilted in favor of speech: rather the reverse. Even for so unmusical a thinker as Freud, it is the musical element of speaking melody that makes it compelling.

In his reconstruction of the experiences behind his famous "Revolutionary Dream," the analysis of which takes up several discrete sections of *The Interpretation of Dreams*, Freud recalls humming Figaro's defiant aria "Si vuol' ballare, signor Contino" from Mozart's *The Marriage of Figaro* after witnessing some imperious behavior at the railway station by the reactionary minister Count Thun. The words not uttered establish a frame of reference. But it is the music, into which the words have been absorbed, that carries the force of impudence, resentment, and rebelliousness. Freud's text quotes the words, but the reader who eyes them without hearing the music in the mind's ear will miss more than half the point. The hearing even has to go beyond the melody per se to the way it was performed. Freud is a little dubious that anyone else at the station would have recognized the familiar tune, implying that he may have been humming it off-key or with some other changes that would indicate his resentment. In other words, he was in all likelihood distorting the tune under the pressure of his feelings. The distortion forms a surplus of expression, a remainder, that marks the rage of a liberal against political reaction and a Jew against anti-Semitism. Meanwhile, the melody per se identifies Freud with Mozart's Figaro as a figure of triumphant impudence, and perhaps also with Mozart himself as a figure of resistance by genius to aristocratic privilege.

The same balance of force and signification occurs every time a vocal phrase is picked up by an instrument or ensemble, whether in an abstract composition, in musical theater, on a movie soundtrack, or in everyday life—Freud was hardly alone in humming, singing, or whistling an accompaniment to events in the process of living them. Film especially, or video more broadly, makes constant use of speaking melody, so much so that it seems basic to video forms not only as an auditory supplement, but also as an element of visuality. One can, it seems, see more, see better, in both the visual and conceptual senses, when speaking melody is somewhere in the picture.

But speaking melody is not a neutral form. Whether because it involves the absence of word and voice, or because its historical development connects that absence with the imagery of disembodiment and the uncanny, of distance in time and remoteness in space, speaking melody above all exists in a modality of pathos. It is nostalgic; it suggests mourning and memory; it hangs on to bits of the past that need to be let go. In so doing, it acts like a material-aesthetic form of "melancholia" in the classic psychoanalytic sense of clinging to the past by internalizing lost objects and reproaching them inwardly for the loss they represent. Of course, this is only a tendency, not a law. It is not hard to find exceptions. But the tendency is strong: no law, but perhaps a rule, a model with a long shadow.

Freud's dream analysis is a case in point because it does seem like an exception: "Si vuol' ballare" is defiant, not mournful. But in Freud's account it is really both, its aggressiveness a scant disguise for political and personal nostalgia. The melody harbors a longing for the hopefulness of Freud's happy childhood in the time of the liberal "Bürger" [Bourgeois] Ministry of which he writes elsewhere in the dream book. "It began to dawn on me," he says there, "that [another, thematically related] dream had carried me back from the dreary present to the cheerful hopes of the days of the 'Bürger Ministry,' and that the wish that it had done its best to fulfill was one dating back to those times." Symbolized by the pleasure-ground of the Prater, the famous park on the city's outskirts, the Vienna of the 'Bürger" Ministry conjoined the love of Freud's parents for their son, a fortuneteller's prophecy of a great future for him, and the hope of full assimilation for Austria's Jews.[4] Without the loss of that fair early world, the music in the latent content of the "Revolutionary" dream is pointless. Figaro's defiance at the train station is the hopeless defiance of an exile in his own land.

What gives speaking melody such power? Freud's narrative suggests that one answer lies in the gap between the expressiveness of the melody and the meaning of the words. The words tell us, or would if we could hear them, what the melody says, but the message thus delivered is always incomplete. We know that the melody in the slow movement of Mahler's First Symphony is saying "Frére Jacques" or "Brüder Martin," and saying it glumly, but what we are to do with this information the melody does not say. If one subtracts what the words say from what a melody expresses, there is always an expressive remainder, a surplus or excess to deal with. And that remainder is the heart of the matter. With sung melody, the remainder tends to be veiled by the fullness of voice; speaking melody takes the veil away. How does this remainder act, and to what end?

The short answer is that it acts by distorting the texture of ordinary reality—the lifeworld governed by the norms of law and language, Lacan's symbolic order. It does so either to create an incitement to new acts of symbolization or to insist on the presence of something unsymbolizable. To continue with the Lacanian vocabulary, the remainder is either an enhancement of the symbolic or an eruption of the Real.

Žižek's model concerns the latter. His essay "Grimaces of the Real" focuses on the human face as a primary locus of symbolic reality and examines how the Real—the terrible enjoyment of living substance devoid of rule or reason—makes its appearance by agonized facial distortion. Many of Žižek's examples also involve the voice, which produces a grimace when it cannot come to utterance. The voice in such cases is an object that gets stuck in the throat; it is "what cannot burst out, unchain itself, and thus enter the dimension of subjectivity," which is also the dimension of symbolic reality. "The first association here," writes Žižek, "is Munch's Scream . . . [where] it pertains to the very essence of the depicted content that the scream we perceive is mute, since the anxiety is too stringent to find an outlet in vocalization. . . . [This] structural muteness is indexed within the painting itself by the absence of ears from the homunculus's head: as if these ears, foreclosed from the (symbolic) reality of the face, return in the Real of the anamorphotic stain the form of which recalls a gigantic ear."[5] Ana/morphosis: form carried backward, form formed again as deformation, deformity. The remainder of mingled desire and repulsion left over by any act of symbolization here returns by indelibly disfiguring the act of symbolization itself.[6]

But not all remainders are anamorphotic stains. An alternative type is one of the topics canvassed by my book *Musical Meaning*. Consider again that one of the commonest notions about music is that one can't express what it means in words; something, and the most important thing at that, is always left over. Yet these musical remainders have nothing monstrous about them; quite the contrary. And the scream in Munch's *The Scream* looks like the very antithesis of music. So what would happen, I wondered, if instead of treating the musical remainder as either an ineffable *je ne sais quoi* or as a negative principle, an abstract curb on articulate meaning, we tried to regard it as a positive phenomenon, a concrete involvement with the problem of meaning?

The remainder in that case would not be what disqualifies me from speaking about music or from finding new contexts in which the music becomes meaningful. On the contrary, it would be the rationale and the motive for me to keep on speaking and contextualizing. The remainder would deny a portion of meaning in the present only in order to promise it, though never all of it at once, in the future. The anamorphotic remainder that impedes the hermeneutic would be joined to a metamorphic counterpart that promotes the hermeneutic. And these two different remainders would actually be one and the same.

Of course texts and pictures have such remainders, too; the grimaces of the Real have opposites in every medium. What makes the musical remainder special? And what, more particularly, is special about it in the case of speaking melody?

Where the Real appears, there is probably no point in making distinctions; all the remainders are breaks in the skin of perception, whether they are blots, garbles, or noises. But where meaning hovers just out of reach, distinctions are possible. The hermeneutic remainders of texts and images are relatively abstract and immaterial, the faint traces of the unsaid or unseen. Our everyday confidence in the force of meaning rests to some degree on this faintness. In music, however, the remainder is material and sensuous. Grasping the remainder is fundamental to both musical pleasure and musical power. Music does more than "have" a remainder; it embodies its remainder. Indeed, one way to define music is as the material-sensuous remainder of interpretation.

Speaking melody is a hybrid of the musical and verbal instances; it combines the material consistency of music with the symbolic value of words, but without merging them together as sung melody tends to do. In the sphere of utterance, the remainder tends to appear as a reduction of articulation to pure phonic substance, intonation denuded of speech. This reduction, like the remainder itself, is subject to a duality whose tensions determine its precise effect in any given instance. On one hand, the reduction may occur when words are choked back, garbled, smeared together; at its outer limit, this verbal implosion would be the equivalent to the sickening distortions of face and voice described by Žižek. On the other hand, intonation may simply replace all or part of a speech act as an overflow of some immediacy or nuance; its distortion would be hermeneutic, at worst enigmatic, and at the extreme a token of intimate, virtually unmediated communication. There is, of course, an endless variety of mixed instances between the two extremes.

Speaking melody belongs to this intermediate domain. Or perhaps one ought to say that the intermediate domain belongs to it. When a melody allows us to apprehend the words we do not hear, it acts as a detached form of the intonational substrate of speech. The process is like an unveiling of the living substance of the words, the rich materiality that the articulateness of speech regularly obscures. Like the words themselves, this substance is purely virtual. When the unuttered speech is incorporated in the sensory richness of the music, the music tends to assume the status of the terrible but fascinating Real, the unsymbolizable kernel of forbidden/ecstatic pleasure/repulsion at the core of subjective life. Beneath any specific distortion that may mark this effect lies the innate distortion produced by the simultaneous occurrence of verbal understanding and verbal absence, which renders the music palpably but imperceptibly different from what it would otherwise be. The notes aren't different; the melody is. Each of these distortions magnifies the other. This mutual resonance helps explain the emotional force of speaking melody.

But the Real thus made manifest is not the standard Real. Rather it is a Real partly recuperated for the symbolic order, a Real allowed to enter the symbolic as something other than a blot or grimace. This other or, so to speak, lyricized Real does not repel meaning; on the contrary, by assuming an aphoristic, enigmatic, oracular character it attracts meaning. Speaking melody undoes the grimace of the Real. Its anamorphotic remainder fuses with its hermeneutic remainder. Speaking melody gives the Real a haven in reality.

Žižek's descriptive terms—blot, stain, smear, grimace, let alone phallic anamorphosis—are too extreme in this context. Speaking melody typically trades in slighter distortions, shimmers or flickers of misperception; if the distortion is too great, the speaking melody turns into travesty—for which, of course, there any many uses—and becomes a device of alienation, as, once again, in Mahler's "Frére Jacques." We need a term for the distortion characteristic of speaking melody, so I will speak here not of blot but a blur, something at the edges of perception rather than "in your face": the smudge of the Real.

The effects of this smudge are best understood in relation to the persistent melancholy that haunts speaking melody. What kind of melancholy is it? And why do we court it?

To answer, we need to ask a further question: In speaking melody, who is it that speaks? The voice, which is unheard, has no tone, no timbre, no material identity; it belongs to no one, especially not to the one who hears it. This voice is not a person's but a persona's; it issues from the music as if from behind a mask (which is the first meaning of "persona"). This is clear enough in the case of Freud, who ventriloquizes in the voice of a rebellious persona compounded half of Mozart and half of Figaro. The "voice" of this compound ghost is not only the specific speaking melody of "Si vuol' ballare" but also the figurative voice of Mozart's music in general, the voice of the Enlightenment against which the authoritarian figure of Count Thun stands in reactionary opposition. But the ventriloquism works in reverse. It is not so much that Freud speaks in the voice of this Mozart-Figaro as that he lets its voice speak through him.

But again, what voice? Whose voice? As we will soon see, and no doubt would have predicted, the persona who speaks in speaking melody comes in many forms. But its identities do have an underlying consistency, and one consistent with the penumbra of melancholy and loss that most often calls speaking melody forth. Perhaps the best way to unmask this hidden speaker is to call up its closest relative, the voice of conscience or law or, in Freudian terms, of the superego.

That conscience speaks is one of the oldest of Western tropes; that law acquires voice through conscience is both a legal principle and a theological one, the speaking law, *lex loquens*, forming (in early modern legal theory) the site of union between secular and divine authority;[7] and that the internalized lawgiver, the superego, derives from things heard is an element in the Freudian trope that Freud explicitly recognized. Common to all these figures of the law within is the understanding that the voice of conscience is a voice of admonition; it accuses, it reproves, it demands. A good conscience is a quiet conscience. Those who hear voices in their head are tormented by them. A voice without a body is at best uncanny, at worst intolerable.

Except, that is, in speaking melody. For just as speaking melody gentles the Real to a smudge, so it softens the voice in the head that tells us we've only gotten what we deserve. Speaking melody, even at its most melancholy, speaks as we would want it to. If, as Freud suggested, living for the ego means being loved by the superego, which itself lives above all to withhold that love, then speaking melody allows us the illusion of love granted. Where accusation was, commiseration must be. If, Freud aside, we live under the dark supervision of the *lex loquens*, then speaking melody remakes that law without repealing it. Confronted with Count Thun, Freud turned the voice of authoritarian rule against its own real-world embodiment and, in so doing, joined his embrace of Enlightenment liberalism with aesthetic pleasure.

One final point to take from these observations: Neither the smudge of the Real nor the pathos of speaking melody is merely a general effect, an abstract artifact of theory. Such general effects are never, or let's say rarely, realized in their generality. They respond, rather, to particular circumstances; they mark their materiality, their distortion, and their nostalgia in highly particular ways. That, in fact, is what makes them interpretable, what brings them into the field of meaning. Mahler's version of "Frére Jacques" or "Brüder Martin" (would that be Martin Luther?) is a whining, hiccoughing funeral march, the "external stimulus" for which, according to the composer, was "the parodistic picture, known to all children in Austria, *The Hunter's Funeral Procession*, from an old book of children's fairy tales."[8] Speaking melody is both a historical form in itself and one that insists on rather than insinuates the historical character of its particular realizations. We might even say that one effect of speaking melody is to prevent melody itself from taking flight into the illusory sphere of the nonhistorical.

A useful profile of speaking melody must therefore be historically resonant. To meet that requirement, I propose to examine a series of examples spanning several media across two centuries: an opera and a movie from the 1940s, and a pair of instrumental compositions from the 1820s.

The opera is Britten's *Billy Budd* (1951). In this adaptation of Herman Melville's novel, Billy, the innocent "Beauty" or "Baby" aboard a British man-of-war, is falsely accused of mutiny by Claggert, the master of arms. The accusation may be a distorted form of Claggert's desire for Billy, which must not be symbolized; Billy, who stutters under stress, replies in distorted form as well, striking and inadvertently killing Claggert in lieu of speech. Remainders are thus at the heart of this story, which ends as the ship's captain, Vere, orders Billy's execution despite his obvious innocence. The order is given in anguish; Billy's last words are "God bless Captain Vere!" Britten and his librettists, E. M. Forster and Eric Crozier, were primarily interested in Vere, whose dilemma is exposed early in the opera by means of speaking melody.

Talking with his officers about the danger of mutiny, Vere draws attention to a chantey being sung below decks as the crew retires for the night. He takes the chantey as a sign of contentment; it is exactly the opposite. The words express a deep longing to be elsewhere, anywhere but here: "Blow her away, / Blow her to Hilo, Hilo, Hilo. . . ." At the end of the scene, Vere, now alone, is distracted by the chantey as he tries to read. The song is already halfway to becoming voiceless, smudged by the distance of its off-stage, below-decks source. Part of it is submerged in the darkness of the low voices singing together. Part of it fades into the distance with the repetitions of "Hilo," which turn the exotic place-name into pure vocalization, more smudge than utterance: a becoming-inarticulate of speech under the pressure of desire.[9]

The metamorphosis completes itself a moment later as the orchestra picks up the chantey and makes it the basis of an extended fantasy. What is truly at stake becomes fully apparent when the fantasy takes up the speaking melody of a second chantey, introduced on solo flute. The words will not come until later. Britten wrote this tune before he had words for it—words, he told their author, that should be "as gloomy, homesick, and nostalgic as you like."[10] The words he received convey a deep longing for release, even for the peace of death: "Over the ocean, over the water, into the harbour, carry me home." Taken together, the two speaking melodies universalize the feelings of which they speak. The men's longing ceases to arise from the circumstances of the narrative and becomes the circumstance from which the narrative arises. The longing becomes manifest as the unfathomable substrate that the opera, at best, can symbolize only in part.

To complete the picture, we might observe that *Billy Budd* also includes the mirror reverse of a speaking melody: a "melody"—it never quite becomes one—for words that are spoken but never heard. The music is the mysterious series of so-called interview chords that takes the place of the unshown scene in which Vere and Billy alone speak face to face. The bond between these two is a love indifferent to class, age, learning, and law. We can say of this love that it mingles the spirit of Christian *agape* ("charity" in the Pauline triad that begins with faith and hope) with a Platonizing homoeroticism in the spirit of Oscar Wilde (still an iconic figure when to be gay in Britain was to be an outlaw): "a deep spiritual affection that . . . repeatedly exists between an older and a younger man, when the older man has intellect, and the younger man has all the joy, hope and glamour of life before him."[11] Above all, however, this love is, precisely, a mystery, and its mystery is what the chords most strongly envoice: what they show without saying. The key *to* the chords lies in not worrying about the key *of* the chords. Trying to hear their underlying tonal sense is a refusal to listen; they are floating triads in pure colors—no more, no less—as innocent and inexplicable as Billy himself. They sustain their mystery until the very end, when a "plagal" cadence (but it is not one) emerges: F-C-F-C-D-C. When the progression ends the scene shifts to Billy in chains alone, awaiting execution. The penultimate chord, D, is the dominant of the dominant, G, whose place it takes. The substitution makes what is unheard, the elliptical dominant, the most important chord of all, the inaudible equivalent of the spoken word, both of them heard more acutely in their silence than they could ever be in the their sound.

Just a few years before *Billy Budd*, Hollywood produced a legendary instance of speaking melody in *Casablanca* (1942). The story has become legendary, too: Separated when the Nazis occupy Paris, the lovers Rick and Ilse (Humphrey Bogart and Ingrid Bergman) meet again in Casablanca; Ilse is now married to a resistance leader, and Rick must renounce her so that she, in turn, can support her husband in his struggle. The song "As Time Goes By," as sung at the piano by Rick's employee and emotional minder, Sam (Dooley Wilson), embodies the lost romance.

On separate occasions, first Ilse and then Rick insist on hearing the song, but with a subtle difference. Ilse starts by asking for the music (with the famous "Play it, Sam") but she also wants the words ("Sing it, Sam"). Rick reencounters Ilse for the first time when he interrupts Sam's singing—an interruption that cannot hold up. Alone with Sam later, Rick, too, asks for the song ("Play it!" he says, turning Ilse's plea into an anguished command), even though he can't bear to hear it; we can see as much in the grimace on Bogart's face. But what Rick asks for is speaking melody, not song, and the film complies. As Sam plays, the orchestra backs up the melody before shifting to the underscore for what follows, a flashback to the lovers' life in Paris.[12] Most of this interpolated narrative is fragmentary; music holds it together, especially "As Time Goes By." Fragments of the melody recur as underscore at all the key romantic moments, each more haunted by impending loss than the last. But it is precisely these moments that the song, as speaking melody, is bringing most vividly back to life. When Sam actually plays and sings the song for the lovers in Paris, no one suspects its power to do that.

The flashback ends with a return to Rick, still listening as Sam plays. (The playing breaks off at the musical phrase for "and still say," leaving the music for "I love you" to hover somewhere between something still to be said and something no longer sayable.) Far from just invoking a lost time, the song is what refuses to let the time be lost. That, after all, is what the melody says when it speaks: "The fundamental things apply/As time goes by." The fundamental things are those that remain as time goes by, and in this case the most fundamental thing of all is the song itself. If Rick, if Ilse, could forget the song, they could let the past be past. But they can't forget. The song will not let them; it smudges their every thought with the Real of their love.

The close of the film is haunted by the logic of the song, which it can neither accept nor escape. In the penultimate scene, Rick has firmly resolved to let Ilse go; he will send her away himself. To end the story, he will end *their* story. He explains his renunciation with one famous line after another: "We'll always have Paris," "The troubles of three little people don't amount to a hill of beans in this crazy world," "Here's looking at *you*, kid." As he speaks, the orchestra on the soundtrack weaves together phrases from "As Time Goes By"; when he finishes, the strings fill the ensuing silence with a melting rendition of the song's refrain as the camera lingers on a close-up of Ilse's face. The effect is to contradict the narrative ending. The music's speaking melody puts the audience in the position of the old Rick, the Rick who refuses to let go of Ilse and Paris—a refusal measured precisely by the original version of the song. The quivering strings of the closing version impart the smudge of the Real and create a complex pattern whereby Rick says one thing and the speaking melody that supports him says something else: the very thing he would like to say, but can't. The pattern culminates with an epiphany at the level of speech genre: Melodrama (that is, music joined to the spoken word, but with a play on the sense of highly wrought narrative) resolves itself in lyric.

Perhaps this outcome is why some people go back to *Casablanca* over and over, as if hoping to meet—just once—with the ending announced by the music, not by the plot. The song, of course, has been heard on the soundtrack before, even heard too often, but it becomes decisive here because Rick is repeating the separation from Ilse that gave the song its power in the first place. In this context, the absence of the words becomes the presence of the unspeakable desire that will not permit itself to be renounced. The speaking melody clearly says that the problems of three little people—especially two of them—amount to far more than a hill of beans, even in this crazy world.

A lesser world, if not a crazy one, is Schubert's topic in portions of two major instrumental works, his Octet in F (D. 803) and String Quartet in A minor (D. 804), composed during the same two-month period in 1824. Both works quote a song he had composed five years earlier, "Die Götter Griechenlands" (The Gods of Greece; D. 677). The short text, excerpted from a poem by Schiller, bears full quotation:

> Schöne Welt, wo bist du? Kehre wieder,
> Holdes Blütenalter der Natur!
> Ach, nur in dem Feenland der Lieder
> Lebt noch deine fabelhafte Spur.
> Ausgestorben trauert das Gefilde,
> Keine Gottheit zeigt sich meinem Blick.
> Ach, von jenem lebenwarmen Bilde
> Blieb der Schatten nur zurück.

> Fair world, where are you? Turn back again,
> Sweet blossom-age of nature!
> Ah, in the fairyland of songs alone
> Still lives your legendary trace.
> The died-out meadow mourns,
> No godhead comes before my eyes.
> Ah, of that life-warm image
> Only the shade remains behind.

In both the octet and quartet, the only phrase reproduced as speaking melody involves the two words "schöne Welt" (fair world). But the two works invoke this phrase to markedly different effect. We have to go back to the song to see how and why.

The passage quoted is less "in" the song than appended to it by the piano alone. Repetitions of a single three-note figure, static and forlorn, frame the song proper; they also intrude on it about two-thirds of the way through (see Example 2.1) At each occurrence, this refrain sounds over an unchanging but unstable A-minor harmony—afloat, as it were, in the no-world of the present. This harmony, the tonic six-four chord, literally sets the tone for the entire song. In Schubert's harmonic milieu the chord is a mere semblance; it can never function as a tonic, though Schubert sometimes uses it as an estranged

EXAMPLE 2.1 Franz Schubert, "Der Götter Griechenlands," mm. 1–4, 36–end.

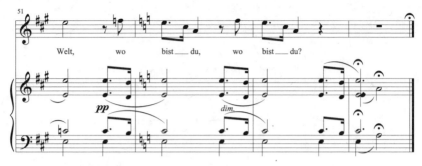

EXAMPLE 2.1 *(Continued)*

surrogate.[13] In context, the chord is like the died-out meadow of the poem, the mark of a fair form made known only through its absence. It is within the frame made by that absence that the song places its lament.

Between the framing statements, we hear a disrupted A B A pattern: two A-major sections enclose an A-minor middle section that ends with the intrusion of the refrain. The first A-major section carries the verse to the point where the gods are said to live on only in song; the A-minor section begins with the transition to the fraught word *ausgestorben* [died-out] and goes on to the end, marking the dismal consequences for latter-day reality. The second A-major section recapitulates the first section's first half, consisting of a double statement of "Kehre wieder,/Holdes Blütenalter der Natur" [Turn back again/Sweet blossom-age of Nature]. This recapitulation is ironic at best, both in its major key and in the incompleteness of its utterance; its structural inevitability only darkens its implications. The invocation is one that can never be answered, as the closing return of the voiceless refrain declares. Deprived of the gods, Nature cannot even say "No." The static futility of the refrain figure expands to envelop the form of the song as a whole.

The rhythmic shape of this figure mirrors that of "Schöne Welt" in the voice, which is, however, sung to different pitches. The speaking melody provides an alternative intonation that is never realized vocally because it is too despairing; its minor mode and harmonic instability too fully confirm the loss that the voice, hoping against hope, still questions with its "kehre wieder." As the song proper begins, the voice cuts across the piano's oscillating E-D-E with the rising figure C-D-E. At first the result is dubious. When the voice and piano coincide on E, it is to the word *Welt,* the term of absence linked to the absence limned in the harmony. The sound is hollow, the apostrophe cast into a void. Yet as if the very enunciation of the word still bore a trace of promise, the voice tries again at "du," the term of intimate communion, and finds an A in common with the piano as the harmony finally shifts, though one can't really say it resolves, to a real tonic triad.

At the end of the song, this balance of hope and despair is lost. The voice reaches its A with no corresponding A from the piano, which is no longer listening, just continuing to brood with unbroken six-four harmony. As if abandoned yet again, the voice has little recourse beyond silence. The piano concludes by repeating its own more melancholy version of the refrain figure. Only after this does the harmony shift again, again not really resolving, and with the voice no longer a factor. In "Schöne Welt," it is the forlorn alternative voice that has the last word, and the true word, in a speaking melody rather than the sung one of which it is the shadow, the shade that remains behind.

It is worth noting in passing that the original version of the song has no shift to root position at the voice's first "du." By adding the shift, Schubert converts its subsequent absence at the last "du" from the restatement of a settled condition to the enactment of a loss. In this context, the deferred concluding shift—call it a lurch—to the root-position triad rings especially hollow. The effect is similar to the more famous close of a later song, "Am Meer," which resolves a mysterious dissonance (the augmented sixth) to the tonic six-four while the keynote, carried over from the dissonance itself, lingers in the deep bass. The result is a harmonic ambiguity that the ear cannot resolve: Sounded over the keynote, the six-four chord is a fiction, but because the keynote is not rearticulated, the tonic triad is a ghost. In "Schöne Welt," the final triad is an acoustic potsherd, the fragmentary token of a vanished whole. It is just the right harmony for the forlorn voice of the speaking melody that, a fragment itself here, sings in this place.

The instrumental quotations in the octet and quartet echo this alternative voice. They do so to especially uncanny effect because their immediate point of reference is not an origin, a sung melody, but only another echo, a speaking melody. As we know, the origin in this case has never been heard at all; it exists only in the melody that echoes it. More than ever, this melody "speaks" in a voice whose question—"Where are you?" or rather, "Where *are* you"—is its own answer, which is "nowhere."

The third movement of the quartet seeks to counteract this answer precisely by catching the little phrase up in its genre, the minuet, an antique form that fulfils the subsequent statement in Schiller's poem that the fair world survives in fable, though only there. The tight, static shape of the phrase acts as a smudge on the richly wrought minuet theme, but the theme has little trouble coping with it. Or rather, just a little; there is nothing glib about the process. The solo cello begins the movement with a deep, groaning statement of the "Schöne Welt" phrase, the last note of which refuses to let go and draws the other instruments to it in somber-hued imitations. But the over-riding lyrical impulse is already at work even as these echoes chime in, and the graceful lilt of the minuet emerges from them seamlessly and irrefutably (see Example 2.2). The smudge is not erased, but it becomes a kind of sepia

EXAMPLE 2.2 Schubert, Menuetto from String Quartet in a Minor, D. 804, mm. 1–11.

tone enriching the gentle melancholy of the old-fashioned dance. If the fair world survives only here, we can still be assured that it survives well enough.

This is an assurance that the octet will not allow. Here the smudge becomes a smear in the guise of wrenching string tremolos that envelop the little phrase (see Example 2.3). The feverish quivering of the ensemble forms an extended slow introduction to the finale, which emerges as an attempt to seek in original composition the consolation that the minuet claims to have found in genre. The movement is superbly equipped to succeed in this. Its indefatigable first theme frames a sonata exposition unusually rich in melodic variety, and the theme itself varies prolifically and irrepressibly during a development section that it wholly engrosses. But the attempt to recall a vanished world by these means is compromised by its very definition. Accordingly the movement

EXAMPLE 2.3 Schubert, Finale to Octet in D, D. 803, mm. 1–7.

EXAMPLE 2.3 (*Continued*)

nearly founders when the introduction returns, briefer but more feverish than before, just prior to the coda. The coda itself seems oblivious, but the listener can hardly be that in good faith. Where the quartet stresses the consolations of fable, the octet dwells on the emptiness of the shades—the ghosts and figments—that the fair world has left behind. Both pieces repeat the little phrase like a forlorn cry, but the quartet follows the text by ritualizing and therefore rationalizing that cry, substituting the generic conventions of the minuet for the rhetorical figure of apostrophe. The octet lets the cry erupt and fade without the intervention of ritual or rationale. Its little phrase is a noisy remainder that the effervescence of the finale cannot assimilate.

The little phrase, then, has larger implications, and not in this one piece alone. What are the larger implications of speaking melody itself? What might its role be in a broader auditory culture?

Let me offer two answers, one based on taking our examples as a sequence, the other based on taking them as a group.

The sequence is logical, not chronological. In terms of the model elaborated earlier, we might say that the voice in the speaking melody at the end of *Casablanca* is the seldom or never (yet) heard voice of the loving superego. That voice arises here only on condition that what it "says" is false, just as the voice of its worldly surrogate, Sam, can be heard only on condition of Sam's external position, as a black man, from the culturally sanctioned narrative of romance. In this respect, the speaking melody of *Casablanca* is the antithesis to those in the Schubert song and octet, which gentle the loss of the "fair world" by voicing it with elegiac regret but also install in the subject who has lost that world a faint, nagging sense of guilt for the loss. The speaking melody heard by Britten's Captain Vere lies somewhere in the middle, because the voice of suffering fraternity that originates in the bowels of the ship becomes the agent both of Vere's moral failure and also of his redemption. The three examples may thus be taken to mark out a hermeneutically useful spectrum of possibilities that they do not, however, begin to exhaust.

On the evidence of our examples as a group, the phenomenon of speaking melody would seem to mark the limit of an important hermeneutic principle, as formulated by Hans-Georg Gadamer: "Language is not just one of man's possessions in the world; rather, on it depends the fact that man has a world at all. The world as world exists for man as for no other creature that is in the world. But this world is verbal in nature."[14] Against this, as an exception to it, is the fact that there are many moments in life when language is silent, suspended, but the world is not. What we experience at such moments cannot be the verbal nature of the world. Rather we must come into contact with something prior to the world as word, cosmos as logos, and yet something consistent with it. We must experience the imprintability, so to speak, of phenomena by language.

For Wittgenstein, a figure missing from this interlude but one to whom we are about to return, this imprintability manifests itself primarily by intonation, the musical substrate of language. We feel it directly when questions of tone—what tone we hear, what tone we're using or should use—catch us up. Consider the situation in which one reads a poem or a narrative with feeling rather than merely skimming the lines for information. The example is Wittgenstein's, who says that in that case, "The sentences have a different *ring*. I pay close attention to my intonation. Sometimes a word has a wrong [falsch] tone; it comes out too much or too little. I notice this and my face expresses it" (*PI*, 214). My intonation is the medium through which language and experience meet, and in terms that I can describe, or at least judge, as true or false to the experience.

Listening to instrumental music often involves a more immediate form of the same awareness. Such listening can suspend language without at all suspending world; rather the reverse, for the music "worlds" us very powerfully. When that happens, we can hear the world's latent imprintability as a positive form, but still prior to the realization of any actual imprint. And this is a condition that shows us the world in a special light, perhaps one less susceptible than usual to rationalization and distanced perception. The world thus disclosed is pleasurably smudged by the Real. Often enough we add to the smudging ourselves by intonation or gesture, a point also noted by Wittgenstein: "We say this passage gives us a quite special feeling [Gefühl]. We sing it to ourselves and make a certain motion in the process, perhaps also have some sort of special sensation [Empfindung]" (*PI*, 182). Although these "accompaniments" make sense only as we listen, they are not, *pace* Wittgenstein, "quite empty except just when we are singing this passage." Instead, they blend the actuality of listening with the potentiality of speech by heightening the intonational matter common to both. In this context we can speculate that what speaking melody does is to make apparent the otherwise imperceptible movement, the crossings to and fro, between symbolic imprintability and the imprint. Speaking melody captures the lapse of meaning by which meaning is replenished, a moment inflected by both reason and magic, both surplus and loss.

NOTES

1. Raymond Williams, *Culture and Materialism: Selected Essays* (London: Verso, 2005), 22–27.

2. On iterability, see Jacques Derrida, "Signature Event Context," in his *Margins of Philosophy*, trans. Alan Bass (Chicago: University of Chicago Press, 1982), 307–29.

3. Jean-Jacques Rousseau, "Essay on the Origin of Languages," in *The First and Second Discourses and Essay on the Origin of Languages*, trans. Victor Gourevitch (New York: Harper and Row, 1990), 282.

4. Sigmund Freud, *The Interpretation of Dreams*, trans. James Strachey (New York: Avon, 1965), 226. The other dream goes by the sobriquet "Uncle with the

Yellow Beard"; its latent content overlaps that of the "Revolutionary" dream in an extensive network of associations. Freud traces his wishes all the way back to his mother's pride, shortly after his birth, at a fortuneteller's statement that she had brought a great man into the world; to childhood revisitations of the scene of the prophecy in the Prater, where another prognostic said that Freud would become a cabinet minister—the image on which the whole pattern converges; and to the hopes for full assimilation of the Jews that the Bürger Ministry inspired: "My father had brought home portraits of these middle-class professional men [of the Ministry]—Herbst, Giskra, Unger, Berger and the rest—and we had illuminated the house in their honor. There had even been some Jews among them. So henceforth every industrious Jewish schoolboy carried a Cabinet Minister's portfolio in his satchel" (225–26).

5. Slavoj Žižek, *Enjoy Your Symptom! Jacques Lacan in Hollywood and Out*, 2nd ed. (New York: Routledge, 2001), 117.

6. Žižek's initiative can be understood as an effort to extract the kernel of truth from the truism that no act of symbolization is ever complete. Lacan defines the Real, to the extent that he defines it at all, as that which resists (evades, escapes) symbolization. Taking this resistance psychoanalytically rather than metaphysically, he understands the Real as pertaining to (being "of") the subject's unspeakable desire. Žižek regards the Real as a kind of agency, and a powerful one at that. Rather than forming a negative, indiscernible limit on the power of the symbol, it intervenes continually in symbolic processes, marking its presence obtrusively with its signature stain or deformity. And because these extrusions of the Real are indeed linked to desire, they can never be escaped. For Žižek, reality (the symbolically constructed world) is pockmarked by them.

7. See Peter Goodrich, "The New Casuistry," *Critical Inquiry* 33 (2007), 683.

8. Quoted in Donald Mitchell, *Gustav Mahler: The Wunderhorn Years* (Berkeley: University of California Press, 1980), 157; the source was *Picture Book for Children* by Moritz von Schwind.

9. Hilo is a port in the Sandwich Islands (that is, Hawaii), as remote as possible from the Atlantic setting of the opera. On another reading, the nonsense that "Hilo" becomes through repetition makes another kind of sense. In the opera's Anglicized pronunciation, it forms a synoptic statement, unrecognized by the singers, of the social (and would-be metaphysical) difference mapped onto the ship's decks: high/low.

10. Mervyn Cooke and Philip Reed, *Benjamin Britten: Billy Budd*, Cambridge Opera Handbooks (Cambridge: Cambridge University Press, 1993), 65.

11. Oscar Wilde, *Intentions* (Mobile Reference [Google E-Books], 2008), n.p.; accessed June 6, 2011. Wilde's remarks form part of his reply, at his trial for sodomy, to the question "What is 'The love that dare not speaks it name'?"—a question that may have resonated for Forster and Britten in the construction of *Billy Budd*. For a more detailed account, see Philip Brett, "Salvation at Sea: Britten's *Billy Budd*," in *Music and Sexuality in Britten: Selected Essays,* ed. George E. Haggerty (Berkeley: University of California Press, 2006), 70–80.

12. Berthold Hoeckner has drawn attention to the song's transitional role here and to its eventual embedding in the flashback it introduces; see his "Transport and Transportation in Audiovisual Memory," in *Beyond the Soundtrack: Representing Music in Cinema*, ed. Daniel Goldmark, Lawrence Kramer, and Richard Leppert (Berkeley: University of California Press, 2007), 163–83. Hoeckner's reading sees lost time less fatefully than mine does, but there is no need to choose between them; the two readings deal with different modes of memory.

13. For example, in the song "Einsamkeit," from *Winterreise*, also a lament for a lost world, the song twice comes to a kind of inverted climax by cadencing from the dominant of C major to a pianissimo pair of C-major six-four chords (or, to add further uncertainty, to the first-inversion triad over a dominant pedal). The phrase to which this occurs is, tellingly, a snatch of speaking melody echoing the phrases "*Luft so ruhig*" (air so peaceful) and "*Welt so Licht*" (world so bright).

14. Hans-Georg Gadamer, *Truth and Method* (5th German ed., 1986), trans. Joel Weisheimer and Donald G. Marshall (revised 2nd ed.; New York, 1989), 441. The first part of Gadamer's statement is a paraphrase of a statement by Heidegger in the latter's "Hölderlin and the Essence of Poetry" (1939), in *European Literary Theory and Practice*, ed. Vernon W. Gras and trans. Douglas Scott (New York: Dell, 1973), 31.

THREE

Expression and Truth

EXPRESSION IS COGNITION.

HOW DO WE KNOW THAT AN EXPRESSION is true, and true to what? The first sign is that something "lights up" with a sudden flare, turning the ordinary act of seeing-as or hearing-as into an event, a call for or piercing of attention. When this happens, some sensory details emerge as tangible centers from which meaning radiates in all directions, sometimes anchoring in other meaning-investments and sometimes just resonating without destination. "Meaning" in this context is not yet a play of articulations but an involvement sustained by the reception and return of these numinous particles. Meaning appears first as the possibility of meanings: those that may or may not come, that need to or need not come—meanings at a distance.

Such numinous particles are, to vary a formula of Stanley Cavell's, both known by feeling and felt by knowing.[1] It is this dual process that raises the question of truth, which is always a twinned question, a two-part invention. The question asks what feeling has known, what knowing has felt. The answer is always more than we could have foreseen. ("Schöne Welt": A short phrase with a lot in it, these words we hear without hearing amid the frenetic trembling that begins and intrudes on the finale of Schubert's Octet. The music keeps repeating the speaking melody like something both baneful and precious. When the phrase lights up, it both pleads with us and assails us. Something very like this may happen even if the verbal allusion passes us by; the virulence of the little phrase is hard to miss.) The answer is felt and known in the question but also suspended there. The answer is promised but veiled, promised in being veiled. Before the answer can be given it appears, tangibly, as the dimension of truth that Heidegger calls its un-truth: the truth not yet delivered or presented—the truth in waiting.[2] (Why the loud stammer that comes and falls away over and over: SCH-SCHöne Welt"? What is the stammer saying—and not saying?)

Failing these events, set somewhere between perception and sensation, the question comes already settled when it comes at all. The answer may be true in a limited sense, but it is a false answer to the question posed. Instead of numinous particles, we get formulaic tokens. The change of *-as* and aspect remains mere repetition. To be truly a question of truth, the question must be unsettled, in every sense. Expression seeks to become true by unsettling the question.

Thus these numinous particles both dazzle and bedazzle us. They call us into their confidence yet also call for an understanding that they defer: In other words, they call for interpretation. This doubleness or self-division— really a twinning, as we have begun to see already and will see more and more—turns on the mutual unsettling of expression and truth. The numinous particles of expression claim our fidelity to them by claiming their fidelity to their source. But how can we get beyond their shimmering to a neutral apprehension of what they express, precisely so that we can judge the expression's truth to it? Doesn't the very idea of "fidelity to" imply an impossible separation of expression from what it expresses?

The short answer is: No. The source of the expression is not a single, bounded, locatable feeling or idea, but the full ensemble of the circumstances, narratives, practices, and prior and future acts of expression of which the expression partakes. The question of fidelity remains productively unsettled as we expose ourselves to this ensemble, to what we might think of only half-metaphorically as the music of this ensemble, which is not a representation of the world but the medium of our inhabiting it.

When expression dazzles, it creates the impression of truth on its own. When it bedazzles, it also withdraws (but the two actions are often simultaneous, often the same action): To reach the conviction of truth, expression relies on interpretation. It does so despite, and by means of, the fundamental condition that interpretations can be neither true nor false.

To recognize this is not to relegate interpretation to the limbo of relativism or pseudo-statement, but, on the contrary, to situate it *in relation to* truth and falsity as a specific mode of cognition with distinct powers and limits. Interpretation cannot offer truth but it can demonstrate what truth might be like. Interpretation is the supplement of truth. It becomes both possible and mandatory (though perhaps not both at once) precisely where fact, however determined, must be incorporated into the sphere of choice, discourse, human significance, the arena of contending values. This is not to deny that fact is always already impregnated with value, but to mark out a sphere of determination, priority, authority.

What interpretation can be in place of true is just what expression can be in the same place. An interpretation can be true *to* its object in a much stronger sense than the familiar one that keeps real truth at a distance. The interpretation that does this is not a mere echo or repetition of its object but the object's iteration in a different register, the object's patient but not credulous interlocutor. Such an interpretation can render a true likeness of its object. It can be true, can become true, not in an unconditional sense but precisely in light of the conditions that frame it. It can become imaginable as what would be true were a truth available. It can add itself to (and so transform) the ensemble of imaginable truths that comes to surround anything we describe and re-describe, perceive and re-perceive, as a piece of our history and culture. It can be true for a while, long or short, then not, and then true again in a different sense.

Truth in interpretation is not a surrogate for unconditional truth but the form that truth takes in a world where truth in its unconditional sense, truth as the one and unchanging, is no longer available. The fact that the truth may alter alters the classic concept of truth, but it is this very openness to change that permits truth to endure the loss of its enduringness. Truth in this conditional sense lives by interpretation, which is thus in yet another sense prior to truth.

The measure of this quality of lifelikeness, of animation, is expression, the expression that beckons almost irresistibly but still leaves room for an act of consent. That room, that space of possibility, is the locus of the bond between expression and truth.

Both Heidegger and Derrida understand truth in the Western world as historically determined by the interplay of two concepts: the truth of description and the truth of revelation, truth as *adequatio* and truth as *aletheia*.[3] On the one hand, truth arises in the conformity of thought to the way things are, the states of affairs by which, as Wittgenstein famously said, the world is everything that is the case.[4] On the other hand, truth arises as the uncovering of the being of things in the fundamental ontological relationships that permit them to be in the first place and to persist in historical time. Either way, truth is essentially conjoined with both dissimulation (it is concealed behind mere appearance) and disclosure (it is what may appear to us, what may become apparent).

But what if there is a third alternative? What if the appearance itself is taken as part, intrinsically a part, of that which appears? What if not only that which appears, but *that* it appears, and how it appears, belong to the substance of truth? What if truth always consists in or attaches to an event of understanding? What if the truth that a certain understanding has come about and must be reckoned with in a certain here and now is itself the model or form of truth more generally?

How can this be known to have occurred, that is, known to be other than mere misunderstanding? How does its claim on us express itself?

The best available answer would appear to be: By the way the event of understanding shows itself *as* an event. "Event" here has the strong sense elaborated by both Derrida and Alain Badiou: An event is something "impossible," something that occurs in excess of its necessary presuppositions. The event neither reveals truth nor corresponds to it. The event *becomes* truth, or rather becomes the condition of its possibility, what Derrida would call its "im-possibility." For Badiou, the truth of the event consists entirely in one's fidelity to it.[5] For Derrida, one's fidelity shows itself in an openness to "the other [that] is always another origin of the world."[6] We experience—should experience—this openness as a form of self-exposure, and the fidelity that goes with it as an encounter with "the very thing that you . . . did not avoid, or could not not avoid (does this come down to the same thing?), and therefore takes the form of the ineluctable."[7]

This reconception of truth as a function of the event is not a simple divorce from the great classical conceptions of correspondence and revelation. It is also a transcription of them into different registers: With correspondence, *adequatio*, fidelity to what is becomes fidelity to what happens; with revelation, *aletheia*, the event of disclosure becomes the truth disclosed. To say this is not to criticize but to specify the register of the event. But this register as described by Badiou and Derrida is nonetheless too epochal, too sublime—not too "impossible," but too rare. Such rarity makes truth inaccessible in the realm of everyday rationality and its twin, everyday fantasy, in which most of life is lived. So the real question of the relation between expression and truth, of the force of expression as descriptive realism, must be settled in the space of ordinary enchantment, the event of every day.

Franz Rosenzweig, writing in the 1920s, sought to settle it there. For Rosenzweig, the event marks a break, not with possibility, but with generality. The event is "the most particular thing there is." It befalls and sustains us in the singularity of our being, the remainder in us left behind when all "predicates" (positive qualities) have been subtracted. The event manifests "neither the *arche* nor the *telos* but . . . rather the singular . . . not beginning nor end, but *center of the world*."[8]

Nonetheless, for Rosenzweig too the event remains exceptional. It stands as a manifestation of divine love, as a penetration of eternity into time. Despite his memorable image of the center of the world, Rosenzweig has not found a way to bring the event fully into the world, nor to give the acts of living that fill the world a numinousness that belongs to them alone. If there is really to be what Cavell calls a quest for the ordinary, for the ordinary as luminous, peculiar, uncanny, touched with enchantment, then all the transcendental language, all the apparatus of the sublime, has to be pared away in the last instance. Radiant immanence cannot be displaced transcendence.

There is no need for that, nor is there need to deny that the sublime sometimes happens. The apparent closure of transcendentals is actually the opening of the ordinary permeated by expression. Under that description, expression sustains the ordinary (or perhaps even creates it) in the form of the common but vital truth of continuous aspect change. Each change has the chance, of course not always taken, to fill with numinous particles the place vacated by the rare or exceptional. The ordinary thus comes to foster (as Eric Santner puts it) "at least potentially, an everyday way of being in the *midst of life*, being open toward the passionate and often enigmatic insistence of what is singular."[9] I want to be able to refer the end of *Tristan und Isolde* not (only) to a dream of self-knowing oblivion but to a bare, half-accidental touch in the dark. I want to be able to refer the culmination of Beethoven's *Heiliger Dankgesang* not (only) to a dream of redemption but to some utterly immanent blessing, to the warmth, at last, of the sun on my cheek or the back of your hand on the sill.

In the event of understanding, the excess of advent over anticipation *appears* in tangible form, and in memorable form. It appears, occurs, and makes itself known, in and as the force of expression in two inseparable senses of "force": force as effectivity, force as bearing; force of action and force of thought.

For that force to take hold, two conditions have to be met. We, who are asked or invited or enjoined to partake of the understanding, must be open to its appeal, sensitive or vulnerable to it.[10] We must be subject to (but not subjugated by) its agency. And to find the force of expression in the event, in whatever verbal, visual, auditory, or mixed form it presents itself to us, we must be capable of interpreting what addresses us, to find an expression that gives back but also transforms—that paraphrases, tropes on, extends, revises—the expression that accosts us. The truth of the event can only appear, and only as through a veil or translucent glass, to the one who takes account of it, the one who can give (and does give) an account of it.

Under these conditions, the interpretation *of* an expression and interpretation *by* that expression coincide. They become mirror images, specular doubles, twins, not indiscernible but inseparable. Each becomes the means of recognizing the other, of recognizing itself in the other. Expression shows the truth it becomes; truth becomes the expression it shows.

In a passage written (in English) in the 1930s, Wittgenstein pins some philosophical reflections to the experience of hearing a piano piece by Schumann on the gramophone; we will take a close look at this passage in the final chapter. Meanwhile (suffice it for now to note), it is striking to find Wittgenstein contemplating the gramophone at all because his work is conspicuous for its lack of reference to modern technology. His descriptions of language games tend to invoke primary materials and simple machines—bricks, word, inclined planes, levers—and he seems to imagine a world in which all communication takes place as (or on the model of) face-to-face speech. Aside from film, briefly mentioned in *Philosophical Remarks*, the gramophone is virtually the only device of modern communications mentioned in Wittgenstein's work. (The telephone does ring once, somewhere, but as if there were no one to answer.) If technology is a leitmotif in Benjamin and a constant subtext in Heidegger, it is almost an unconscious in Wittgenstein.

In a sense, this exclusion is traditional. Philosophical questions about both meaning and sense experience have customarily been posed in terms of a direct encounter between the human and the natural, that is, an encounter imagined as unmediated. But Wittgenstein's gramophone immediately intrudes the question not only of mediation but also of media.

Sound recording has several histories: one linked to moving images, one to public spaces, and one to itself alone. Taken by itself, sound recording severs expressive sound from its source. From the Edison cylinder to the LP, the CD to the iPod, recording has been a technology for producing disembodied sound. Until the turn of the twenty-first century, such disembodiment carried with it a spectral, uncanny dimension that nothing could quite overcome, and that no one quite wanted to overcome. Recording installed a gap between sound and source that retroactively affected expressive sound as such. Music, voice, and speech all lost the indivisibility that once was inherent in them but could now only cling to them as a filmy residue. If, as Žizek suggests, reality qua the symbolic order is inevitably haunted by spectral forms in which the unsymbolized Real returns[11] (the mirror inversion, we might speculate, of the stain or the smudge that is the Real's other venue), recording provided a space for the specters of sound to haunt. These acoustic specters are the means by which the exiled source returns, by which the sound's source becomes its echo.

Recorded sound has always already vanished; the recording preserves both the sound and its vanishing. The most evanescent and arguably the most essential elements of expression survive—the intonation, the vibratory contour, the inflection—but only in estranged form, disengaged from the living source that alone could have produced them. The attachment that we may form to a favorite recording may well involve a desire, a fantasy, a pathos of reanimation that comes as much from ourselves as from the source. We will have more to say about this when we turn to Schumann—numinous particles of Schumann—on Wittgenstein's gramophone. But in the meantime, things have changed.

What happens when the material source of sound recording is not an object but a digital file, played back not on a machine set apart from the listener but on a miniscule device fitted right to, or right in, the ear? Held close to the body or worn on it, these devices are small enough to serve as acoustic prostheses, sensory extensions of a cyborg self moving discontinuously throughout a constantly changing, nonlocalized, decentered network. Delivered direct into the ear, the expressive sound is neither embodied nor disembodied, not because the sound is something else but because the categories are no longer relevant.

Does expression in this non-framework become inexpressive? Are we confronted with a higher-order version of the loss of aura famously (too famously) described by Walter Benjamin in the 1930s? If the uncanny becomes the normal, can another uncanny take its place? Can we recover the enchantment of the expressive by returning to the face-to-face encounter, stripping ourselves of our prostheses the way lovers strip themselves of their clothes, or is the face-to-face encounter itself inevitably altered by this epochal change in the human sensorium? What does it mean even to ask?

> Each moment
> Of utterance is the true one; likewise none are true.
> Only is the bounding from air to air, a serpentine
> Gesture which hides the truth behind a congruent
> Message, the way air hides the sky.
>
> —John Ashbery, "Clepsydra"

Not "*a* true one"; *the:* because truth is absolute. But the absolute truth is that a truth can be absolute only in its moment, the passing moment when its possibility comes to pass. But possibility in expression, in the moment of utterance, assures that no truth is the only truth, so that—yes, it is true—no moment of utterance is true, except perhaps to itself. No interpretation is necessary. Yet that an interpretation is possible *says* something necessary. Possibility in each moment of utterance is another name for ontology.

And so it is that the moment of utterance recorded in Ashbery's text both is and is not the true one; that the hiding of the truth is a revealing ("the way air hides the sky"); that the absence and presence of truth form a likeness in the poem's speech, each becoming the figure of the other; that this confluence is not an impasse but a condition of the movement—the bounding as both leaping and boundary-drawing—that makes the truth as elemental as air or sky; that the language of the text plays truly on "from air to air" as the music we hear and the stuff we breathe; that the verse slithers around the serpentine as both fatal, mystical (the symbol of eternity, the snake that swallows its own tail), and beautiful (the S curve or curve of beauty in eighteenth-century aesthetics and landscape architecture, the movement of indirectness or *différance* celebrated by Derrida); that, among other congruent messages, Ashbery's image of the air hiding the sky recalls—it's the truth!—Wallace Stevens's observation that the imagination adds nothing to any scene except itself;[12] that the truth is not the transparent and the transparent is not the true.

Seeking a metaphor for the paradox of musical expression—nothing could be more exact, nothing could be more elusive—W. H. Auden finds himself falling back on the poet's recourse, grammar: "If I were a composer, I believe I could produce a piece of music which would express to a listener what I mean when I think the word *love*, but it would be impossible for me to compose it in such a way that he would know this love was felt for *You* (not for God, or my mother, or the decimal system). The language of music is, as it were, intransitive."[13] This intransitivity is the source of the traditional vertigo that overtakes thought about music; to put it in Wittgenstein's terms, we have no familiar grammar of intransitivity, and because we do not, we misconstrue the suspension of reference for the absence of meaning. Intransitivity too is a mode of cognition, and one we should learn to paraphrase, for it is the means by which music seems to put us in touch with what we value most, desire most, recall or hope for most. Auden's case is exemplary. He loved music, especially classical music, and his poetry is full of references to it, but he does not know how he knows by it. What he does know, but without knowing how to proceed, is that we cannot stop with the idea that music expresses only itself.

The music expresses itself. Wittgenstein once said as much in his most sustained reflection on musical expression, a passage we will examine closely in the final chapter. His aim was to counter the idea that musical expression (or, indeed, any expression—as so often, the one models the other) is crudely referential. He too values what Auden called intransitivity. He does not want to hear music as a form of secondhand experience, a bad Platonic copy of an original state of mind that would otherwise elude us. Well and good; neither do I. But does Wittgenstein also mean to drag in the stage prop of musical autonomy, the received idea that music in its essence is absolute and self-referential?

Not at all. His point is that the music and what it expresses are inseparable, so that hearing or performing a melody as such—his standard example—and grasping its expressive content are one and the same action. "In most cases," he says, "if someone asks me 'How do you think that melody ought to be played?' [that is, played with the expression appropriate to it], I will, as an answer, just whistle it in a particular way, and nothing will have been present to my mind but the tune *actually whistled*."[14] The expressiveness of the melody thus is, or always may be, coextensive with a quality of action. But Wittgenstein, for whom language is always language in action, immediately rules out the predictable conclusion that in thus expressing itself music expresses *only* itself. "This does not mean," he writes, "that suddenly understanding a musical theme may not consist in finding a form of verbal expression which I conceive as the verbal counterpoint of the theme" (*BB*, 66–67). That last phrase is only half a metaphor: The speech act and the musical act enter into a performative mutuality that is as much musical as it is verbal. One expression shadows and mirrors another, in a relationship whose acoustic quality is underscored by the element of tone that is always assumed to be present and active whenever Wittgenstein speaks of language.

This does not mean (to echo the text) that music does not constantly elude clumsy referential equivalents. The counterpoint of verbal and musical expression follows a certain logic, though not always consistently. To get at it, we can go back to the idea that we can't recognize "soulful expression" from rules. All right then, how do we know it when we hear it?

We tend to receive expression as successful precisely when it sounds other than referential. Music becomes a bad copy of something else when the music annoys rather than pleases. When we like what we hear (when we make ourselves open to it), the music informs or permeates what it expresses and so expresses something other by expressing only itself. Recall Wittgenstein's little tale of the "reflective Chopin" and the tone-deaf guest. The guest becomes resentful because the music sounds to him like a copy with a secret original or a message he cannot decipher. The host enjoys the "reflective Chopin" because he understands that the reflectiveness is not something the music signifies but something it releases, fosters, or models by becoming true to it as an event of understanding.

Expressiveness arises when the perceived qualities of a communicative performance become those of a subject position, which is to say, of a subjectivity that can be assumed. What qualities, and how assumed, are endlessly varied; what remains reasonably constant is the access of reciprocity between sensing and selving and the felt presence of that access itself as a part of the expressive situation. Expressive performance is the form of action that possesses these characteristics. Expressive composition, in all senses of the term, is the form of design that concretely establishes the possibility of certain expressive performances.

Expression may or may not communicate the state of mind of a particular historical actor. What it always communicates is a way of inhabiting a world. Each act of expression, therefore, in varying degrees that may be highly charged or scarcely noticed or anything in between, potentially asks for assessment on the same grounds that world making stands or falls on: value, meaning, and truth.

Music is the expressive universal, or as close to one as we have. At some time or another, nearly everyone is moved by musical expression. But if Wittgenstein is right (and he is), we are not thus moved by hearing either something "in" the music or something the music refers to, but by hearing the music *as* something. To hear musical expression is to hear music as something more than mere sound. It is to hear this more-than-sound while hearing the musical sound acutely. Musical expression consists of making this surplus available.

But to avail ourselves of this expression, we must also contribute to it. The surplus is not something we find but something we impart to ourselves in listening-for, in hearing-as. In some cases, this is just a matter of recognizing conventions, in the same way we do when we encounter a classic speech act. But being moved by musical expression is not the same as merely recognizing it, and the difference lies precisely in the perception of the surplus investing or invested in the music. This surplus is not *what* the music expresses—it cannot be reified that way; instead, it is the being-expressive of the music.

But musical expression does not end with its perception, and that it does not is part of what constitutes it. The music in moving us moves us to express its expressiveness. Most commonly we do this by compressing the music into a momentary trope in a parallel medium: by bodily movement, by exclamation (a sound or a word, perhaps a phrase quoted from memory), by mimicry (we sing or whistle or hum), by visualization. These reactive, or more properly proactive, expressions are interpretive acts. They have a cognitive value that can be developed into descriptions or into more fully interpretive, that is, hermeneutic language. Such language, which is (and must be) expressive in its own right, seeks to disclose what is at stake in the reciprocal experience of expressive and re-expressive hearing-as.

But what holds good for music holds good for expression in general, of which it is the paradigm. Gesture, stance, and motion, tonal fluctuation and the vocalic stream, the display of color and outline, all present themselves "musically" to be perceived as things endowed with a surplus over their material presence. And that surplus always has cognitive value. It professes to make a truth known—or to make a truth.

The laws of musical truth are those of a certain fluid dynamics, as if our lives as speaking subjects were bathed in a palpably charged atmosphere, filled as if by a subtle lyrical matter that ebbed and flowed with our speech acts. (Early modern science, mingled with speculative philosophy, hypothesized the real existence of such a substance mediating between matter and spirit.)[15] Recognition of this shows up in a metaphor that occurs to Wittgenstein as he asks about the relation of meaning and feeling, the pursuit of which leads beyond metaphor to something stranger:

> When longing speaks out of me saying "If he would only come!" the feeling gives the words "meaning" (Bedeutung). But does it give the individual words their meanings?
> But here one can also say: the feeling gives the words *truth*. And so you see how here the concepts flow into each other. (*PI*, 146)

The sentence in question belongs to a distinctive type we might call the expressive performative. It is a performative utterance insofar as it enacts a self-exposure or self-revelation, that is, expresses the longing that impels it. When we hear, "If he would only come!" we are supposed to hear it as wrung from the speaker by longing. But this occurs only insofar as the feeling behind the sentence is real; the feeling makes the utterance constative in being expressed. If the feeling is lacking or fictitious, the sentence may still be true to the *concept* of longing, but only, and precisely, as a performance of it in the sense of an actor's performance, a mimesis. Without the feeling, the sentence will not verify itself.

The difference is often a fine one, even in "real" situations (and for that matter, in dramatic ones). The way we can tell the difference, if we can, is by the tone of the utterance. What is real has its own sound. From that sound, its imitations always have a certain distance, even if it is minute; that distance itself is a form of truth. "When one says, 'I *hope* he'll come,' . . . the feeling perhaps gives the word 'hope' its special sonority (Klang); i.e., it has its expression in the sonority" (*PI*, 146). No sonority, no hope. The tone is the medium by which the feeling gives the words truth. Its quality as experience conforms to Wittgenstein's fluidic metaphor: Expression and truth meet like two currents joining into one or two waves intermingling. Their truth sounds in their music and their music comes from their truth. It happens, so to speak, electrostatically.

This is not to say, however, that the utterance merely makes apparent what is already intrinsic to the feeling. The words give the feeling effective as well as affective reality; they constitute part of the feeling they are moved to express. The feeling not only gives the words truth but also assumes from the words the concrete delineation of the truth it gives. Even though the words derive their meaning from the situation as well as from the feeling behind them—the encounter is not a closed circle but a swirling confluence—they convey a great deal just on their own. In that sense, Wittgenstein's apparently rhetorical question about whether the feeling gives the individual words their meanings has a surprisingly affirmative answer. The sentence that prompts the question—"If he would only come!"—is both subjunctive and incomplete. It must be uttered of someone who may or will or cannot come, or who may come too late, and it must be uttered of someone the consequence of whose coming is so fully clear that the "then" to its "if" clause may freely be suspended. (The suspension is also a part of the meaning of the missing clause. The clause is *better* left suspended.) Such a sentence is to be wrung out on a breath, and it must be uttered in a certain tone which, we might say, is no less a part of its grammar than the words in their order. Such a sentence is one that may be "wrung from us—like a cry" (entringen—wie einen Schrei; *PI,* 146). For all these reasons, it is laden (geladen: loaded, charged) with the wish it expresses. And this is *not* a metaphor.

These considerations throw new light on the idea that feelings, emotions, moods, and the like are cognitive, and that the expression of them must therefore be cognitive too. Drawing on neuroscientific models of brain function, Antonio Damasio hypothesizes that emotions are "somatic markers" of the situations that provoke them.[16] Once moved in a certain way, we see things differently, and in most cases see them better than we could otherwise. There are many situations that cannot be well understood without taking account of the feelings appropriate to them. We reason with such feelings; we interpret with them. But we most often do so in proximity to expressive performatives, the force of which radiates through our language generally and completes the confluence of expression and truth.

One function of music is to ritualize the experience of that confluence. Just as an expressive performative like "If he would only come!" condenses in itself the drama of expression and truth with respect to the many possible circumstances in which one might say the sentence, so a passage of music condenses that same drama with respect to the many possible sentences that the music might inspire or intimate or model. One sign of this is the audible gap that separates music from any text sung to it, the gap that underwrites the possibility (historically discovered rather late) of independently expressive instrumental music and that gives vocal music its special sonority as doubly laden with the burden it expresses. Like the expressive performative again, music can tell us most when heard amid the confluence of its circumstances, but it can also tell us a great deal just on its own. We can always hear it as something, and almost always do. For all these reasons, music is part of the fundamental grammar of culture. Its relationship to the confluence of expression and truth is not accidental but essential.

Long ago, in graduate school, I lived near a horn player. On fine sunny summer mornings, but never on other days or in other seasons, he or she (I never knew which) would greet the day by playing the horn call that ushers in the finale of Brahms's First Symphony after a troubled introduction. The sound filled the little street on which we lived, so much so that it seemed a part of the scene and a part of the weather; it was never possible to say just where it was coming from. The player clearly had a story to tell, and I have been composing narratives for it ever since.

When used to make a specific reference, the term *music* usually designates a pattern of pitches and rhythms capable of being reproduced indefinitely, with or without variation, in several media: a score, a series of performances, recordings. The kernel of permanence, the configuration that survives intact in every reproduction, is what we name when we name a piece of music or, indeed, refer to a segment of music as a "piece" or a "work." Whether we actually hear the pattern as such, as in classical composition, or only in a series of family resemblances, as in popular song, is significant generically but not ontologically. And even the generic difference is not absolute.

But this pattern or kernel is a strange phenomenon, the strangeness of which has long been dulled by our habits of reference. The vaunted pattern has no fixed location except insofar as names or definite descriptions provide the fiction of one, yet it seems quite definite. In some sense it doesn't "exist," yet we can encounter it, interact with it, and understand it as if it did. The identity of a "piece" of music is actually like identity itself as conceived by Judith Butler, a series of repeated performances, some of them only fragmentary[17]—performances that encompass not only "performance" in the musical sense of realizing a score, but also arrangements or transcriptions together with their own performances and variants, plus citations, adaptations, recordings and their playback, mental listening, singing or humming in everyday life, and so on.

Contrary to Butler's strong nominalism, however, the music thus produced is no mere fiction or phantom. It has an ontology; it just doesn't have a tangible form. Nor is it a purely "imaginary object," as Nicholas Cook calls it, at the same time as he eloquently captures the conjoined elements of pathos and desire in music's fragile effort at "snatching eternity, so to speak, from the jaws of evanescence."[18] Music, rather, belongs in the numerous company of objects that have no stable material embodiment but are nonetheless brought into existence as intentional forms once they cross a certain threshold of cultural installation or investiture. Such objects include literary, dramatic, and legendary persons (from Hamlet to Sam Spade), places (ancient Rome, Dickens's London), and things (the *petite madeleine*, the picture of Dorian Grey). They also include music, the most immediate yet most elusive entity of the kind, something realized as itself, not as a representation, yet something more intangible than any representation.

Recognizing this mode of existence is important in part because it alerts us to the ontologically open character of music, its capacity to reshape itself as meaning in different material and cultural environments. It is important in part because this mode of virtual existence is at odds with both empiricist and materialist worldviews—but not with their strengths: the former's emphasis on scrupulous observation and the latter's refusal of supernatural appeals. And it is important because it indicates music's affinity with tangible objects that have been ontologically heightened by acts of symbolic investiture or endowment, the practice of which cuts across the difference between material and nonmaterial forms.

The sheer ordinariness of this phenomenon also points up something important about both music in particular and symbolization in general. Both show an impetus toward sublimation in the Lacanian sense of the elevation of an object to the status of the Thing—the primordial and unattainable object of desire that stands beyond signification "at the core of human activity."[19] "Amid the forest of desires and compromises" that comprise that activity, we only ever approach the Thing through its surrogates, which we perceive as more than they are. But this process cannot escape its own activity; it bites its own tail; it is always getting above itself. The elevation of the object also operates in the field of the ordinary (not the banal: the ordinary, and not the banal just because the process operates). At times sublimation just gives the object a little lift, in much the way speaking melody employs the smudge rather than the stain of the Real. The forest of desires has its clearings. There is a "middle style" of symbolic endowment that goes on there, an ontology of the actual, which becomes the arena of practical spirit without pushing to the sometimes destructive or heedless limits of the sublime. Equipped with this conception, and joined by the real things covered by it, we can hold the everyday open to numinous particles, to aspect changes brushed by animation, to enchantment without magic. This is the equivalent in everyday life of the use of interpretation in intellectual life as the countervailing force to both empiricism and dogmatism.

Shelley describes being moved by the expressive power of music "'Till joy denies itself again / And too intense is turned to pain" ("With a Guitar. To Jane," ll. 7–8).[20] The experience is one in which music regresses to something like the cry that for Shelley and others of his generation was music's origin. But the elegantly turned couplet with which he evokes the experience, a turn of verse with a music of its own, seems necessarily to contemplate that experience from a distance. Shelley's language can echo the musical effect but not reproduce it because pain cannot be written and the cry cannot be articulated. Unlike music, it would seem, language must maintain an impermeable barrier between pleasure and pain.

Could the eternally troubled relationship between words and music turn in part on this difference?

Is pain antithetical to language? Is the expression of pain, in truth, antithetical to language?

By default, it is. Pain, physical pain in most cases, mental pain in some, expresses itself in vocalizations that are universally intelligible but belong to no code: in sighs, groans, exclamations, cries, screams, wails, grunts, moans, sobs, and so on. Such expressions have a peculiarity that Wittgenstein found compelling. They can be faked, but when they are genuine they cannot be mistaken; we can believe a fake cry but we cannot disbelieve a real one. The expression of pain is the index of a certainty.

Our relationship both to ourselves and to others is partly grounded in the certainty that pain offers. On the one hand, the certainty of pain suggests a revised form of *cogito*: I hurt, therefore I am. From the standpoint of actual life, this version is much more plausible than the Cartesian alternative, "I think, therefore I am." Life offers me few practical occasions on which to doubt my own existence. Under what circumstances would I be likely to need to reassure myself on the matter by checking up on whether I'm thinking? But pain is ubiquitous. It is inevitable that I will often feel the certainty of being the being I indubitably am in feeling the pain I indubitably feel. And it is inevitable, too, that this will lead me to express myself in the language of pain, which is not a language. (Linguistic expressions of pain always seem to carry the penumbra of a possible lie: "I can't, my stomach hurts," "I have a headache," "It still hurts." But the vocalization of pain seems almost to be the model of speaking truth, to be one of the primary forms of our relation to truth. "The suffering person," says Wittgenstein, "is the one who expresses the pain" [*PI*, 101]; no questions asked.) But to whom is this expression addressed?

To the other from whom I seek recognition, who can be any other: any other one. The expression of pain is less important when I voice it than when I hear it. When someone else expresses pain, I come into direct contact with the certainty of *that* person's existence and therefore find myself in an ethical relationship. "If someone has a pain in the hand . . . one doesn't offer comfort to the hand but to the sufferer; one looks into his eyes" (*PI*, 98). This relationship is eminently practical. It does not require an abnegation of my own being in favor of the other's of the sort imagined by Emmanuel Levinas; it does not entail reflection or self-examination. It simply requires that I do something, if I can, to ease or at least to recognize the pain.

Perhaps in doing so I will say something; in the economy of pain language does after all have a place. But I cannot bridge the gap between language and the expression of pain by making a statement. As Wittgenstein remarks, the two do not run parallel:

> Misleading parallel: the scream, an expression of pain—the sentence [Satz], an expression of thought.
>
>   As if it were the goal of a sentence to let one person know how it is with the spirits of another [wie es dem Andern zu Mute ist]: only, so to speak, in his thought apparatus and not in his stomach. (*PI*, 104)

Neither constative nor performative utterances can let one person know how it is with the spirits of another, but that is exactly what the expression of pain does every day.

This train of thought, however, leaves out something important. Is pain antithetical to language? It is so only if we leave tone out of account. But how can we leave out of account something that is never out of action, something without which language cannot speak at all? In speech, in writing, there are accents of pain, and their presence charges and changes the meaning of whatever is said. Insofar as we hear them, they color and intensify the promise of truth that language as such carries with it as a condition of possibility. The accents of pain are like the accents of desire inverted: The one insists on truth while the other insists in truth's despite. But when we pass from simple to complex utterances, from vocalizations and speech acts to discourse, certainty itself begins an irreversible metamorphosis from fact to fiction. Language is constantly in flight from the certainty that grounds it. But it must thus spread its wings if it is to say anything substantial.

Which brings us by a long roundabout way back to our constant point of reference, namely music. More particularly, it brings us back to song and more particularly still to the vast repertoire of sad songs, mourning songs, songs of lost love, songs of lament. This repertoire is so large because it is foundational for the very concept of music; it proves the truth allegorized by the myth of Orpheus from the earliest operas (Peri's *Eurydice*, Monteverdi's *Orfeo*) to Rilke's *Sonnets*:

> We should not trouble
> Ourselves about other names. Once and for all
> It is Orpheus when there is singing. He comes and goes. . . .
>
> O how he has to vanish, for you to grasp it![21]

We can extend the Orphean repertoire to speaking melody and to cantabile melody in its darker vein, but its origin does seem to lie with the singing voice—the voice positioned in the zone where vocalization and language overlap. Song in this dispensation bridges the gap that statement cannot. It becomes the language of pain without ceasing to be language. It becomes the means by which I may not only encounter the other person as a fellow being but also preserve, repeat, and intensify that encounter by the simple act of giving it a contour of pitches and rhythms that may be repeated or varied or both.

But here things get more complicated. The condition of possibility for these expressions of pain in song is normally that the singer not actually be in pain—except perhaps by identifying sympathetically with the pain the song expresses, something that the listener may do as well. Both the singer and the listener may thus participate in the pain without enduring it. This is also likely to be mental rather than physical pain; the melancholy of song is a means of securing the extension of physical into mental pain, not as metaphor but as a direct presentation of self. So in two distinct senses (the pain is not the singer's, the pain has no body), the pain expressed is not real in the sense that the pain of a wound is. Yet in a more important sense, it is just as real as such material pain, only in a different register. It is not a pain one suffers but a pain one assumes. It is a pain that, in assuming, one both interprets and mitigates. Such pain has meaning; and meaning may help relieve the pain it cannot remove. Such pain can be transmuted into or by aesthetic pleasure, into which the direct presentation of self may be extended still further, even if each new extension, though certain enough, is less certain than the last.

Between what Giorgio Agamben calls voice as mere sound and Voice as the bearer of language,[22] melody arises and transforms the terms it mediates. No account of the genesis of meaning can ignore the role of music or its proximity to the expression of pain.

In the right circumstances, every memorable melody is melancholy.

When does expression occur?

One answer is: always. There can be neither speech nor action without expression. The world we live in is expressive insofar as it is a world at all.

Another answer is: at the moment of exception, the moment of turning or transport. "Transport" implies both a state of rapture (becoming rapt, being carried away) and the trope, literally the turning, of metaphor (the Greek *metapherein* becomes *transferre* in Latin).

Paul Celan, in a prose text entitled "Meridian," calls the *when* of this exception, this syncopation, the moment of breath turning. The turning is from inspiration to exhalation. It occurs as the moment in which language becomes poetry by casting itself beyond itself toward an unknown other, in the face of whom (or which) the "I" who speaks becomes more than a historical person fixed by a place and a date. Celan expresses this moment of expression as the finding of a meridian: a noon (the form of the trope favored by Nietzsche; already we are having a conversation), a midnight, and an imaginary circle drawn through the poles and around the circumference of earth.[23]

Derrida, in a reading of "Meridian," dwells on the paradox of the date. To mark an event or utterance with a date, usually coupled with a place-name, is to mark it as a singularity. That which is dated happens just once, once only, in just one place. It cannot be repeated. It cannot return. It cannot wander. Yet that is exactly what it does do. We make its return, its commemoration, its spectral wandering possible precisely by dating it, by keeping its date in mind. The act of dating effaces the singularity it marks; it makes the singularity readable at the cost of retracting it.[24] Expression occurs when we simultaneously grasp the singular through this double motion and find it slip our grasp.

Expression is almost everywhere; expression is almost nowhere. How can these contraries be reconciled?

One answer is: through moments that have no date and—therefore—cannot help but seek one—seek many. We need and accept a world of expressions that disappear as soon as they arrive, but we *want*—in both senses, lack and desire—expressions that preserve themselves through the logic of the date: moments as numinous particles. Such moments occupy a present tense that consists precisely in the possibility of being repeated ad infinitum, the suppositious or virtual condition of the moment's recurrence regardless of what is done and who does it.

Such moments are hard to characterize and impossible to catalog. They have no intrinsic character because until they occur they are purely conjectural. They exist only as the mirages cast by a certain way of thinking or speaking about time. But they do exist, just as, so Celan tells us, despite the stylistic artifice that dates it, the poem speaks. These moments are the artifices of supposition, the counterfactual, the subjunctive, the narrative present. They form the illusion of a primal, more than historical time that is both everywhere and, because it is as intangible as an image on a film screen or the shape of a face in a cloud, nowhere. This time without a date is a tangible emptiness filled with expression; every point within it is on a meridian.

The texts of the later Wittgenstein inhabit this mode of time almost exclusively and form, by indirection, the best available theorization of it. The *Philosophical Investigations* is full of fragmentary parables, numinous particles of narrative and logical tangles, that occupy a time of the ordinary that is also no time at all, any moment and every moment. An almost random sampling:

> Couldn't I think to myself that I had fearsome pains and turned into a stone while they lasted? Well, how do I know, when I close my eyes, whether I have not turned into a stone?—And if that has happened, to what extent will *the stone* have the pains? (*PI*, 97)
>
> Suppose that someone pointing at the sky comes out with a string of unintelligible words. When we ask him what he means, he says it means "Thank

God, it will soon stop raining." He even explains to us the meaning of the individual words.—I suppose he likewise came suddenly to himself and said: that sentence should be full of nonsense, but when he spoke it, it seemed like a sentence in a familiar language. (Just like a well-known quotation.) (*PI*, 145)

"I wanted to say . . ."—You remember certain details. But not even all of them show your intention. It is as if a picture of a scene had been taken but only a few scattered details of it were visible: here a hand, there a bit of a face or a hat—the rest is dark. And now it's as if I knew quite certainly what the whole picture represented. As if I could read the darkness. (*PI*, 163)

The absent minded man who at the order "Go right!" turns left, and then, clutching his forehead, says "Oh! Go right" and makes a right.—What has occurred to him? An interpretation? (*PI*, 139)

Moments like these turn up on virtually every page. The world that they inhabit is fantastic and ordinary at once, twinned in principle, and never otherwise: "And if I say 'The rose is red in the dark too,' you positively see this red in the dark before you" (*PI*, 141).

Wittgenstein tends to think of these conjectural moments under the rubric of grammar, and hence of language, but if they reflect a grammar of sorts, it is at least as much a grammar of time. (The rose is always red in the dark, but you see its red there—and the rose?—only when I say so.) Not *the* grammar of time, as if there were such a thing, but a particular, invested, expressively rich grammar, a grammar of *if* and *as if*, of *what if* and *suppose* to join with the grammar of –*as*, and with only the loosest of ties to the empirical reality that it nonetheless seeks to describe.

In other words, this is the grammar of music. At least it is the grammar of music as Wittgenstein understood it, the classical music whose *if*s and *as if*s ("One says: 'Don't you see, it's as if a conclusion were being drawn,' or 'That's like a parenthesis,' etc.") are meant to be performed at any or every time without deviating—at a minimum—from the pitches, rhythms, and harmonies inscribed in the score. (The rose is red in the dark too.) Another answer to the question about reconciling the ubiquity of expression with its elusiveness is that the reconciliation occurs whenever and wherever there is such music. As poetry in Celan's sense, as the work (meaning the effort as well as the artifact) of art that casts itself rapturously, metaphorically, by the turning of breath toward something beyond itself, the music embodies expression in all its rarity. It vacillates, like the one who wanted to say . . . between scattered details and reading the darkness.

Through the music, expression is slowed to a lapsing away. It still eludes us but we can feel it glide from our grasp exquisitely, in all its detail, as we can feel the contours of flesh glide under our hands. The expression does not simply vanish. Its slow evaporation becomes the ritual of its occurrence through the repeated performance of musical scores. The time of performance is the no time/any time of Wittgenstein's parables; each performance, each work, is a singular event, which is what, since each performance (even the first), is a repetition, is what they cannot be. The performances themselves must be intermittent, so the rarity of full expression is preserved in them. But music as performed presents expressiveness as a universal; no corner of the sound, no chamber of the ear, is untouched by it. (You see the red in the dark before you.)

Music gives the breaking, which is also the blossoming, of the date. For the date, says Derrida, "is mad: it is never what it is, what it says it is, always more or less than what it is."[25] One and the same date may be fraught with significance here, empty of it there; yet the significance can be forgotten, the emptiness suddenly filled. The date is thus—Derrida again: "not an effect of being, of some meaning of being; it is on this condition that its mad incantation becomes music. It *remains* without being, by force of music, remains for song: 'Singbarer Rest' [Singable remainder] is the incipit or title of a poem [by Celan] that *begins* by saying the remainder . . . leaving a song without words (lautlos) to be heard therein."[26]

But the song without words sounds through the words that say the remainder, the words that mark the date, are marked by the date. Turning to the close of another Celan poem, "Cello-Einsatz/von hinter dem Schmerz" [Cello-entry/from behind (the) pain], Derrida falls into a rhythmic incantation, as if saying the remainder were—almost—possible in the tones of melodic speech: "That other poem sets into musical play something indecipherable or unsignifying (Undeutbares). It closes on these words, which say so little, yet more than all, unforgettable thenceforth and made to pass unperceived from memory, in their untranslatable simplicity, their nonetheless rhythmic simplicity":

alles ist weniger	everything is less, than [as]
es ist,	it is,
alles ist mehr.	everything is more.[27]

It is impossible to know what all, what everything, these words name, what date they depart from, what condition they address; they too say both more and less than they say. Their simplicity is the impossibility of their meaning rendered transparently meaningful. The only way to engage that meaning, to participate in and transmit that meaning, is to pronounce these words expressively. They have meaning only in the mouth of the speaker who voices their music and the ear of the listener who hears it voiced. The words on the page form the song without words that wait for the words to be given their song.

Music in the world, music composed and performed, played and sung, embodies this expectation, this offering, this demand, which forms the undertone to every musical occasion. Every one, all: Heard with feeling, any and every music can reveal the more and the less of this condition marked not so much by madness as by the overflow of reason. Music is the affective bridge between expression and the world. If we learn to let it, music will reveal itself—since a bridge runs two ways—as the cognitive bridge between expression and truth.

So to tell the truth, we should sing to each other.

When truth is at issue, and we want the truth from someone, we have to listen closely, to hearken for the ring of truth. If we don't hear this, whatever its tone or timbre, what we hear will in some sense not be the truth, at least not the whole truth.

Yet we have to hear it *in* the truth, not just *as* the truth. Derrida identifies the ethical issue of truth-telling with the impossibility of proving a lie. We may *know* that someone is lying and yet be rendered helpless by the lie's denial. This denial may even be spoken with the ring of truth. So we must also be willing to say that the ring of truth is false when the "truth" being offered to us defies belief. That is the problem of what Derrida would call testimony.[28] The truth has no substance without the ring of truth, but the ring is hollow without the substance of truth. In the end, we must decide, which is impossible, which is, as Derrida would say, precisely why we have to do it.

Classical music, which for right now means written music seeking to be interpreted by intact realization, insists on the madness of the date. This insistence is one of its cultural functions. Inscribed and infinitely reiterable, the score has no date, but the musical work, the eternally unfinished idea only projected or imagined by the score, or scores (in different versions or editions), is an audible transformation of its moment of origin, what Wallace Stevens, speaking of poetry, called "the cry of its occasion."[29] The most important thing about this metaphor is not that it links cry and occasion, but that it separates them. The occasion does not become articulate in the cry (the poem, the music) but through its utterance appeals to be recognized and made known. One reason that classical music is significant as a conceptual as well as an aesthetic resource is that it always balances, almost explicitly, on the knife edge between the date and the dateless, the dated and the renewed.

Wittgenstein asks: "A man may sing a song with expression and without expression. Then why not leave out the song—could you have the expression then?"[30] This is a logical as well as a stinging rhetorical question. The conclusion it points to cannot be stated adequately merely by saying that what is expressed is not independent of what expresses it (hence the two senses of "expression," as both means and end). This is true enough, but it does not reach to the ontological character of the necessary understanding. The expression *of* the song, we need to say, is the expression *in* the song. The expression is not something produced *by* the song but something that the song does in being sung. The expression is something that happens.

This in turn means that the word *expression* is strictly speaking a misnomer. As a trope, the term (the "expression") commonly designates a coming forth, a drawing out, especially of something interior, something shrouded in a subjectivity to which it initially belongs. But as an act, what we call expression would more properly be called an *im*pression, that is, the act takes the stamp, the imprint, of a particular condition; in so doing, it transforms, transmutes, interprets, and communicates that condition; and in so doing again, it imprints that condition on the recipient of the "expression." From there further transformations are not merely possible but likely, even inevitable. This series of imprintings, of inscriptions or transcriptions, along with the preservation of the marks involved (the features that quote, allude to, condense, resignify), is both the meaning and the truth content of the expression.

From this, it follows also that the usual language employed to discuss these topics, Wittgenstein's language notably included, is inadequate. When we say simple things such as "It looks sad," and so on, we are using a drastic form of shorthand. We condense circumstance into epithet. To understand what is expressed we have to reverse this process. The result produces a truth on the Heideggerian model of unveiling, *aletheia*, unconcealedness: When we unpack the substance of an expression, we unveil, disclose or, more properly, rediscloses what expression as epithet has concealed. This concealment, however, is not an expendable part of the process. As Heidegger also says, being, the being of things, reveals itself in concealing itself.[31] We become aware of it as something missed, some part of which is always missing. There is thus always a secretive remainder in every circumstance addressed expressively and in every expression involved in such reckoning. Any account of what is expressed must respect, account for, and preserve, especially preserve, this remainder, because it is the persistence of the unexpressed, the not yet unconcealed, that gives expression a sense of urgency. The unexpressed manifests itself in the drive to expression.

Wittgenstein's mordant question about song also applies to the absurd notion that the hermeneutics of art, and especially of music, is the symptom of a desire to have the expression without the song. On the contrary: The hermeneutic activity is the means by which the song and the listener impress themselves on one another, each one expressing itself in, and in the impression it makes, on the other. The *least* expendable element here is the song.

To act on this recognition effectively requires a whole cultural apparatus. In particular it requires a willingness (also a desire; also a need) to address and preserve certain particular "songs" (and so on) as repositories of expression, the runes of a culture in the act of recreating itself, becoming itself anew in forms both new and old. These values are anything but self-evident and have not always thrived even in the cultures that produced them. But they represent the possibility of preserving the value of singularity and a belief in existential richness in a world where neither any longer has a firm hold, if they ever really did. A culture becomes purely commodified, a culture of expendables, of interchangeable things and people, precisely by approximating the condition of the expression without the song. To be viable, a culture must agree to value, to select and revisit, certain singular forms. These forms are exceptional in themselves, but they are also the guarantee of singularity as a universal possibility.

In other words, a culture needs its song: its melodic speech. Expression is always a matter of music at some level, even where gesture is at stake. If we understand musical expression, we understand expression as such. Or so this book would say, melodically. In its musicality, expression is the performative medium that animates the animate. It is what makes meaning meaningful. That it does these things is the basis of its link to art.

What is perhaps most remarkable about this animation is its ubiquity. Expression is an ordinary occurrence; without it the ordinary would be unrecognizable; it is part of what constitutes the ordinary and even the force that attaches us to the wide field of the ordinary, the value of which, as Stanley Cavell urged us to hear, is one of the great underlying principles of Wittgenstein's later thinking.[32] But of course expression can rise to the extraordinary. Its potential to become remarkable is one of the bases of the concept or practice (the terms are hard to distinguish) of the aesthetic. We will turn to this nexus of the ordinary and its extra-, speech and melody, in the next chapter. For now, suffice it to observe that the artwork puts a frame around expression to uncover its remarkableness and its ontological power. The work turns what in action is a contingent event into an informal ritual. To do so has gradually become the primary role of "art" in modern Western culture since the formulation of the idea of the aesthetic in the mid-eighteenth century.

Meaning and expression are not identical, although they are obviously related. A good way to describe their relationship is to say that I express what I mean but always mean more than I (can) express. The bridge between meaning and expression arises in the form of what I called numinous particles at the start of this chapter. An examination of these will wend its way back by degrees to the presiding question of expression and truth.

Meaning has generally been understood as a conceptual phenomenon, or even as the phenomenon of the concept. My aim is to treat it as perceptual: as an *aesthetic* phenomenon in the root sense of the term *aesthetic*, understood as referring to a historically delimited field of experience born of the European Enlightenment. To shift the emphasis slightly, meaning is commonly situated in the sphere of the signified; the aesthetic resides in the sensory regardless of whether the object of aesthetic interest is rich or poor in meaning. But this dichotomy is untenable, not least because meaning and sensory cognition can virtually never be separated from each other. The question is not their relative presence or absence but their relationship.

According to some recent work of Jacques Ranciére, that relationship takes the form of a neither/nor: The aesthetic appears when what confronts us is neither conceptual nor sensory.[33] This observation turns Hegel inside out (not for the first time!): The aesthetic does not occur as the sensuous embodiment of an idea but as that which neither is nor is not either sensuous or conceptual and that which neither is nor is not the amalgamation of these modes into a unity (sensuous embodiment). This way of thinking is more responsive than the tradition from which it breaks to the conviction, persistent at least since the eighteenth century, that the aesthetic mode is not a product of other forms of perception but something singular, with its own phenomenology and ontology. If so, the fact marks a break or a redirection in the history of perception (which, of course, has a history; perception is not a natural phenomenon except in its material basis).

What would the consequences be of recognizing all this? Ranciére opens the door; what happens when we walk through it?

First, the artwork and its equivalents would be constituted as that which emerges when the sensory and the conceptual are addressed side by side in their neither/nor. This means that the artwork, the thing to which we address our concern, would be neither perceived nor thought. It would be apprehended in a mode for which we have no convenient term.

Second, this mode is not a blank negativity. It has a palpable positive quality; it projects the neither/nor in mirror reversal or turns it inside out. Like all expressive modes, the aesthetic works in the dimension of negativity in the sense that it breaks with the real as such. The aesthetic world is always imaginary even when it takes material form. But the aesthetic equally breaks with the *not* real. Although it is not progressive like the Hegelian "negation of the negation," the aesthetic acts in the syntax of the double negative: the not unlike, the not unknown, the not untrue, the not impossible—all illustrations that are also descriptions of the mode of the aesthetic in its positive form.

Third, some of the language I used previously, "the thing to which we address our concern," is a theory in the form of a description—and again a departure from our customary vocabulary, which would direct the perception of a certain subject toward an external object. That vocabulary is probably inescapable, but it is therefore important to recognize how misleading it is. And to do that requires a gloss on each of the terms in my phrase: *thing, address, concern.* Concern is one of Heidegger's synonyms for Dasein, human being or being-in-the-world; it combines, in another twin modality, concern or care *for* and concern or care *about*, the first involving preservation and tending, the second a taking-the-part-of in excess of personal interest.[34] Things are the material bearers of concern in excess of their usefulness as objects; the excess appears for us in a sense of animation that blurs the distinction between substance and spirit even after modernity has taken that distinction as a default assumption. Concern must always be addressed from one person to another and transmitted by means, paradigmatically the message (letter, speech, or symbol), that may, indeed will, alter both the address and the message in transmission.

I'm inclined, then (to mimic one of Wittgenstein's favored turns of phrase), to propose that the role of expression in the aesthetic field—the field of artworks in more or less the traditional sense—is to give local, concrete, quasi-material form to the neither/nor logic that otherwise operates diffusely across the work. The aesthetic gives this logic its place (the ambiguity of "its" in this statement is deliberate). The combination of concentration and diffusion allows the aesthetic to operate both as mood and as force or act. This dual agency does not form an opposition but a relationship of obverse and reverse: a twinship. Twinship is the positive form of the neither/nor, which disseminates itself through the proliferation of twin relationships.

One of these belongs to expression itself. Expression is one of the twin modalities of aesthetic performance, that is, of the uneven effectuation of meaning in sensory form across the span of the work. Expression reveals or illuminates (it lights up an aspect); its twin, estrangement, puzzles and obscures; it extinguishes an aspect, withdraws from an understanding to re-raise the question of what and whether to understand. (Its role is that of the enigma, which is not the whole modality of art, as Adorno thought,[35] but exactly half.)

Expression and estrangement join semantic performatives (acts of invention or articulation that expressly instate meanings in being enacted) and hermeneutic windows (modes of surplus, deficit, or supplement that call for interpretation in all senses of "call for") to compose the primary formative agencies of meaning.[36] They operate in the twin registers of the aesthetic and the semantic, the twinship of which comprises the field of interpretative cognition. Expression and estrangement do in the register of the aesthetic what semantic performatives and hermeneutic windows do in the register of the semantic.

These two registers, of course, are inseparable, and more, they are never entirely distinct. Each twinship releases meaning in the same way: not as a concept, proposition, signified, or formula, but as a beckoning, a means of orientation for moving in a densely populated, allusive field of concern. It is possible to conceive of these twins as part of yet a further twinning, between an agency that beckons by what it gives or shows (expression, the semantic performative) and an agency that beckons by what it withdraws or veils (estrangement, the hermeneutic window). The whole series of relationships thus belongs to the ontological structure described by Heidegger, in which the truth is also untruth, the twin of which is the formative power of descriptive realism.

To the extent that meaning is dynamic, compelling, or demanding, meaning is an aesthetic phenomenon. Meaning minus the aesthetic is formula— a useful condition that becomes regrettable only when the formulaic is overvalued or mistaken for something more resonant. Meaning becomes aesthetic when it surrenders its conceptuality and enters the condition of the neither/nor.

Meaning crosses this threshold by becoming expressive, that is, by emerging as a tangible rise or fall of qualitative value in point of vividness, intensity, distinctness, inflection, and the like. It typically does so in the form of numinous particles. These are "bits" or consistencies of the meaningful presented with a certain immediacy. These bits are scattered across the surface of the artwork, thick here, thin there, absent elsewhere. They are, however, neither signifiers nor illustrations, though they may *also* be that. They are occasions, stimuli, cues, provocations. I multiply terms here because to get at the aesthetics of meaning, we need yet again to sideline our standard vocabularies.

Numinous particles are details, but what is essential to grasp about them—to say it again—is that they are not clues from which one derives or constructs something numinous, but presentations of the numinous in a particular form or shape. The numinousness gives the details their signification, not vice versa. The situation resembles the one analyzed by Wittgenstein for recognizing faces: When I recognize your face, I do not infer your presence by inferring it from your features. I recognize *you*; it is your face that gives your features their signification, not vice versa.

Underlying this account is the proposal that meaning is a local effect or a scattering or series of local effects that, once established, once perceived, assumes the force of generality and radiates or ripples in multiple directions. "Force" here means primarily illocutionary force, understood as a property not just of words but also of all expressive utterance, gesture, and action. The localization of meaning depends on the occurrence of the semantic performatives that, like speech acts, do in their occurring just what their name announces: they install or release or effectuate meaning.

They do this, moreover, in two senses that always occur together. They install a specific meaning, and in doing that they also install meaning or meaningfulness in general. More exactly, in their general function, semantic performatives reinstall meaning and meaningfulness, or vice versa—neither term comes first—because they have always already been installed, and installed long since; their prior installation is the condition of possibility for the semantic performative itself.

Insofar as the result of setting these forces in motion is aesthetic, the immediate result is the emergence of numinous particles. This does not happen metaphorically (a denial we have met with often: No disrespect to metaphor, that trope of tropes, but we actually enhance its role by narrowing its field). Each half of the term "numinous particles" needs to be taken literally.

The particles are pieces: little bits that exceed or envelop wholes. Their numinousness is not linked to any definite sphere beyond the empirical but it nonetheless constitutes the presence of such a beyond; it is not a sign but a phenomenon.

The particles are material: materialized flecks of meaning. They are not signs, not signifiers; although they draw music into the symbolic order, they are not symbols. They are, as experienced, actions, yet they are also presences, palpable stuff—one could perhaps call them "things" in a semi-Heideggerian sense (in which the vividly resonant thing is opposed to the neutral object), but they lack the generic identity of things (the famous jug for Heidegger, as later for Lacan, a shape that enfolds an emptiness so that fullness becomes possible).[37]

In both respects, numinous particles escape the standard categories and configurations of meaningfulness. They even escape the standard modes of perception. They are not identifiable with any of the forms in which they appear, musical or otherwise, but let's stick with music: They are not melodic reiterations, motivic shapes, rhythmic contours, instrumental textures, or the like, though they may appear as, and need to be described (albeit "under erasure") as particular and particulate occurrences of these things. When they occur, they precipitate themselves out of the categorical field from which they emerge; they are events, singularities, or intensities that are neither in the operative category nor outside of it. Recall the "interview chords" from Britten's *Billy Budd*, which can stand as the example par excellence: each chord with its own orchestration, its own timbre and texture, each, as it happens, incorporating a note of the F-major triad but in such harmonies (does the word *harmonies* even apply?) that the triad is disembodied as the series unfolds. The chords neither progress nor go nowhere; they are neither "tonal" nor "atonal"; they are "chords" only because we do not know what else to call them.

This neither/nor position is the basis of the question of truth raised and unsettled by numinous particles. What one hears is not a sensory form that has become numinous, but a numinousness that breaks into sensory form: What one hears is the ripple of meaning, which concentrates or expands itself into the particle of sense and pleasure.

This process remains pretty well unexplored, though one might argue that it is indispensable to any sense of being part of a world where concern is possible. Music and musical performance are its paradigms; they are the art of making numinous particles. Much as musical interpretation, as I argued in *Interpreting Music*, is the paradigm of interpretation in general, the expressive force of numinous particles in music is the paradigm of expression in general. When Proust singled out the "little phrase" from the sonata of the fictional composer Vinteuil, he was making, in the little phrase "little phrase," a numinous particle that condenses into itself a whole history of musical pleasure and musical memory, of haunting melodies and tunes in the head, of music that impregnates recollection and becomes a form of self-possession.

The interpenetration of sound and memory allows Proust's protagonist, Swann, and the narrator whose memory interpenetrates with his, to

> picture to himself the extent [of the little phrase], its symmetrical arrangement, its notation, its expressive value; he had before him something that was no longer pure music, but rather design, architecture, thought, and which allowed the actual music to be recalled. This time he had distinguished quite clearly a phrase which emerged for a few moments above the waves of sound. It had at once suggested to him a world of inexpressible delights, of whose existence, before hearing it, he had never dreamed, into which he felt that nothing else could initiate him; and he had been filled with love for it, as with a new and strange desire.[38]

Even though Swann is not particularly musical, his "passion for a phrase of music" (the phrase "little phrase" will come later) allows him to "reconsecrate" a life that had become barren. No wonder that there has been a concerted effort to find the "real" little phrase—the numinous particle of numinous particles—in the music of Fauré, Saint-Saens, and Franck. Proust himself said (but he did not always say the same thing) that the Vinteuil sonata was "composed" from elements found in Wagner's *Parsifal*, a Ballade by Fauré, Franck's Violin Sonata, and "a sonata for violin and piano [no. 1] by Saint-Saens which I'll hum for you"—the source of the little phrase.[39]

Perhaps we can agree that the principal locations of expression are face and voice. Not coincidentally, these are also the principal locations of song. (This is not to slight the body, stance, or attitude, but to suggest yet another twin formation.) Expression is thus intimately bound up with the twin ontology of face and voice: of face as the criterion of the human (recognition and perhaps responsibility begin with faces); and of voice as the criterion of the subject (the face brings me presence; the voice brings me sentience).

As Wittgenstein observes, facial expressions are immediate indices of understanding. But when do I produce them? Primarily when something pierces the net of ordinary attention: Facial expression most often arises when one is startled, surprised, caught unawares.

Numinous particles in music have no one format, but they often participate in the logic of the face. They both form the musical equivalent of a facial expression and call on the listener or performer to "face" them, to attend to them with the force of coming face-to-face. Latent in all expression is an act of personification, the giving of a countenance to countenance the expressive act. To the extent that we hear or play music as expressive (a very large but not unlimited extent—that has to be acknowledged), we put a face to it; we hear a face. (And yes, we sometimes see voices.) But the faces involved, real or imaginary, actual or metaphorical, are not those derided by Deleuze and Guattari as instruments of "faciality"—the mechanism that curbs the flow of feeling and meaning with the contour of a coercive mask.[40] These faces don't just put a good face on things. They seek to involve the face as the scene of exposure, of disclosure, of appearance as risk. This need not happen with great drama or fanfare—often the reverse; it happens whenever the flash of a particle makes us turn our heads.

At which point, we are likely to express ourselves. Since faces are at issue, so is what faces do. Numinous particles form the substance of expression—musical and otherwise—in two senses. First, we apprehend them as expressive, as the locations of expressivity. Numinous particles proffer the neither/nor of the aesthetics of meaning. Second, precisely because of that, we receive numinous particles as a call to *become* expressive: to gesture, move, make faces, vocalize, or speak. We become expressive to connect with the expression addressed to us. We acknowledge, we recognize, we participate. Numinous particles revive the dead metaphor of a "striking" occurrence or appearance. These particles provoke us because they pierce our defenses; they get under our skin; they shock our sensibility. By responding in kind, we parry the shock. (I know: This language sounds like Walter Benjamin. Wait just a moment.)

We do not parry to discharge the shock or to ward it off, but to engage with it. We expose ourselves to the shock in order to live out its implications in a kind of dance, an impromptu ritual. When we listen to music over and over we ask it to accost us again, to verify that the shock, the rain of particles to the Danae of the ear, remains unexhausted. Wittgenstein acknowledges this process in a sentence striking not for its suspect metaphor but for its typography and grammar: "In all great art there is a WILD beast: *tamed*" (In aller grossen Kunst ist eine WILDE Tier: *gezähmt*).[41] The elegant italics tame the wild capitals, but only after dwelling indeterminately within the open span (both space and moment) invoked by the colon. What captures *us* in this relationship, which Wittgenstein goes on to compare to that of a ground bass and a melody, is neither the wild nor the tame, neither the thrust nor the parry of shock, but the interval between.

This interval showered with numinous particles has a logic that, like the interval itself, extends the aesthetic "ground bass" of the neither/nor. Although arriving in this middle space ("in the midst of life") is something we often represent with tropes of syncope or rupture or rapture, of being carried away, we are not simply lost or nullified there. On the contrary: Only in the disorientation of that interval do we find meanings by which to orient ourselves. We are not carried *beyond* meaning but so fully *into* it that for a vertiginous moment we may no longer recognize it. Think again of Schubert's "Schöne Welt" figure, that dark version of a little phrase: always wrong in whatever place or form it appears, and we have to expose ourselves to its wrongness (its stabbing, smearing, or trembling) to get ourselves right.

My description of this process in terms of "striking" and "shock" deliberately recalls Walter Benjamin's celebrated notion of the "shock defense," the parry of consciousness to the thrust of surplus perception, as a symptom of modernity.[42] But the resemblance comes with a difference. I do think of this particular exchange as typical of art music from the later eighteenth century on, so much so that I would take the music as a model rather than seeing it first arise, as Benjamin does, in the poetry of Baudelaire. But I do not see the process only as a defense or a desperate remedy. It is also, as the previous paragraph may already have suggested, a primary venue for sustaining the possibility of meaning in the modern era. Meaning in the interval of numinous expression is an animate and animating force. To experience it that way helps keep meaning from ossifying into a useless object, a formula, a bland signified. Meaning is *not* a signified. Or rather, the moment meaning becomes a signified, it is dead.

Wittgenstein famously opened the *Tractatus* with the sentence, "The world is everything that is the case." But it isn't. The world is not the material environment, nor the material cosmos. It is not even the Heideggerian version, the space of the mutuality of things. The world is everything that is *as if* the case. It is the non-totalizable sum of the possibilities of modeling, describing, and imagining it. It is the site where expression and truth interpenetrate—on their best days.

Here is the text of a dream, noted on a stay in Brittany in the summer of 1998. We were sleeping just under the slope of a roof, so the movement of the dream reverses that of the way to the bedroom. I saw a series of Greek chorus or hieroglyphic figures in patterned and stylized dance movement, but with a chiaroscuro suggestive of art deco. There was also a voice-over: "The other disappears. This is the last moment, for those who can [unintelligible], in which life can be perfect." This either preceded or followed a descent on a winding stair; during the descent, the word *percephonic* flashed across my mind: a portmanteau combining *Persephone* and *perce-oreille* (French for "earwig," literally, "pierce the ear") that I had coined for a chapter I was working on at the time.[43] The stair wound down through galleries of erotic/pornographic sculpture to a cabaret-seeming performance in which the chanteuse, after being clutched to the thighs of her partner, sat laughing because her scarflike garments kept slipping away, revealing the erotic "boundary zones" of her body.

None of the zones remained a focal point; what did was the singing. The erotic glimpses each constituted a classical instance of the Lacanian *objet petit a*, to be superseded by the singing as the more compelling and (thus) elusive object. (The *objet a*, object/cause of desire, stands in for the elusive Thing we cannot help but pursue at any cost.) What the dream seemed to be saying at this level is that music at its most suggestive (in the sense of both evocative and seductive) is or unfolds the *objet a*. But what does this mean, and why should the dream's "theory" be taken up in waking life?

A concept like the *objet a* is needed to explain the nexus of intensity, bodily energy, abjection, and rapture that informs the relationships—each and all of them—between the subject and the field of its encounters. Like all psychoanalytic theories, this one is compelled into existence to explain the compulsiveness of human action, the excess of such action over either rational or irrational self-interest. And this leads us directly to music (in a large sense that includes musical visuality and discourse on music) and to music's special ability to "drive people crazy"—since it is precisely being crazy for music, or for someone's music or music-making in particular, that becomes preeminent in the formation of modern (mass?) subjectivity. Music sanctions craziness and gives it a public forum; craziness curbs the impulse of musical form to excessive rationality and in so doing assumes a rationality of its own in tandem with the music. Music, too, precisely because of its spillovers into visuality, discourse, memory, and bodily movement, is a fertile field of the excess required to fill the otherwise empty place of the *objet a*, to form a bandbox full of virtual *objets a*, the formal causes of desire rendered as objects.

Music in excess, music as excess, the remainder always left, always produced, by every instance of music's intelligibility and appropriation; music as the trace of the Real left behind as the calling card of the escaped *objet a*: How is its working to be theorized?

Well, one might circle through the fantasmatic quality of ideology, suggesting how the remainder mediates between social reality and representation; or one could consider the cultural poetics of the remainder, pursuing its effect on the circulation of social energies; or one could focus, like Žižek, on the remainder as unsymbolizable and hence manifest mainly by blot or distortion in the symbolic; or one might explore the relationships of the remainder to systems of power and knowledge in the spirit of Foucault; or one might dwell on the contradictions between the overall sense or effect ascribed to the music and the heterogeneous, conflicted, unstable signifying and expressive processes snagged on the remainder.

Each of these alternatives is attractive. What all of them presuppose is the recognition of music as the dynamic, systolic-diastolic, animate and animating element in the field of communicative performance, something most readily apparent when music intermixes with nexus of texts and images. The musical remainder is thus something that manifests itself less as a quality or an object than as a force. There is always a perspective from which the music insists on something that just won't mix, won't compute, that won't, so to speak, play. And this is not at odds with the meaning, intelligibility, or use of music, but in sync with it, even its condition of possibility. To exist expressively, the music insists on the other side of its expressiveness. This type of insistence is one of the principal means by which the modern Western subject seeks to individualize itself both within and against the sphere of collective life.

How does music appear to us? We have to be concerned with the question; if the fact that something appears is part of the link between expression and truth, the way that something appears must be likewise.

We hear music, of course, and hear it as this or that in a resonating present—Wittgenstein's luminous *Now* (see Chapter 1). But we also play music, see it made, coax it from devices, read it from notation, give voice to it, perhaps compose it, and so on. The strange thing, though, is that in every case we seem to apprehend the music in excess of its medium. Unlike texts, pictures, and films, music seems to have no substrate in which it is inscribed, depicted, or screened. It's made of air. It is a procession of acoustic images or mirages that both envelop and suffuse us.

That last sentence says more than it seems to. Music's ethereality has traditionally encouraged a kind of conceptual synesthesia; we tend to think about music via visual metaphors of space, surface, and scene. The underlying figure seems to be that of a page or other plane that serves as a container as well as a substrate. What we hear there, as if by seeing there, is supposed to be directed either by an underlying structure or design or, in more recent thinking, by a signifying aim. But what if our understanding of expression balks at this picture? What would happen if we stopped thinking of music visually and tried to describe its way of appearing as an auditory phenomenon?

For one thing, the space or surface of music would not resemble a plane; its ground of appearance would be undulant, twisted, looped, curved, multidimensional. For another thing, the procession of sound shapes (let's not call them "images" here) would defer to neither an underlying structure nor an overarching signification. Music is as music does. That's what we can learn from applying descriptive realism to how it appears. The inner workings of music, if we must have the metaphor, become pertinent where—if—the space or surface opens a threshold to them; the meanings of music are wrested, not borrowed, from signification. The auditory surface is less something the music has than something it is, the extension of a sonorous event driven by care, desire, and the logic of aspect-change. In music, we might say, the ideal of a numinous ordinary becomes available with maximum concentration and minimum reservation.

The *objet a* rustles across the musical surface like a voice from the distance that invites and evades our answer, But it seems to come closer (now intimate, now extimate) when the surface undergoes twists in acoustic topology, when it—the surface (but also the *objet a*)—folds, furrows, expands, contracts, distorts, or metamorphoses. The surface is thus the material form and the material presence of the musical subjectivity assumed by the listener so disposed or so seduced.

At the same time, the musical surface is the form and material presence of that impersonal drive energy that threatens to disorder the subject and turn it against its own socialization. Musical expression, like expression generally, lives within earshot of the Real. (Take that horn call from Brahms's First Symphony: the purity of its tone on the dominant of C major appeals for trust, promises deliverance from tumult and anxiety, but the same sonorous warmth bears a trace of the Real, perhaps only its smudge but perhaps also a touch of its stain.) Much of musical aesthetics is tacitly cast as a defense against this outcome. But the outcome is already present whenever musical expression occurs, for it cannot occur otherwise. Music flings us away in the very act of bringing us back to ourselves. And this is not a paradox or a contradiction but simply the way—an instance of the only way—that we only ever come back to ourselves. It is the way expression reaches the threshold of truth.

NOTES

1. Stanley Cavell, "Music Discomposed" (1969), in *Must We Mean What We Say?* updated ed. (Cambridge: Cambridge University Press, 2002), 180–212.

2. Martin Heidegger, "The Origin of the Work of Art," in *Poetry Language Thought*, trans. Albert Hofstadter (New York: HarperCollins, 2001), 52–54.

3. Martin Heidegger, *Being and Time*, trans. John Macquarrie and Edward Robinson (Oxford: Blackwell, 1962), 257–63; and Jacques Derrida, "The First Session," trans. Barbara Johnson, in Derrida, *Acts of Literature*, ed. Derek Attridge (New York: Routledge, 1991), 141–42.

4. Ludwig Wittgenstein, *Tractatus Logico-Philosophicus*, trans. D. F. Pears and B. F. McGuiness (London: Routledge and Kegan Paul, 1961), 7.

5. Alain Badiou, *Being and Event*, trans. Oliver Feltham (New York: Continuum, 2005), 173–90, 201–11.

6. "From *Psyche*: Inventions of the Other," trans. Catherine Porter, in Derrida, *Acts of Literature*, ed. Derek Attridge (New York: Routledge, 1991), 342.

7. From "Desistance," Derrida's introduction to Philippe Lacoue-Labarthe, *Typography: Mimesis, Philosophy, Politics*, ed. Christopher Fynsk (Stanford: Stanford University Press, 1998), 10. Derrida and Badiou converge on the concept of the event as an occurrence that has to be continued for it to have happened in the first place, but in other respects they diverge sharply. For Badiou, the event sets the terms on which its continuation is possible; for Derrida, the continuation is possible only if no such terms are set. For Badiou, truth to the event is an act of fidelity; for Derrida, it is an act of transformation. Badiou's ultimate model is mathematical, and he claims to have "donn[ed] the contemporary matheme like a coat of armor … [to] undo the disastrous consequences of philosophy's 'linguistic turn'"; for a critique of Badiou's "mathemes," see Ricardo L. Nirenberg and David Nirenberg, "Badiou's Number: A Critique of Mathematics as Ontology," *Critical Inquiry* 37 (2011): 583–614, esp. p. 611 for the quarrel with Derrida and Badiou's statement about it. Badiou perpetuates a standard error by misunderstanding Derridean *différance* as a denial that ordinary acts of understanding are credible.

8. Quoted in Eric Santner, *The Psychotheology of Everyday Life: Reflections on Freud and Rosenzweig* (Chicago: University of Chicago Press, 2001), 89.

9. Santner, *Psychotheology*, 91. The passage Santner paraphrases continues the transferred transcendence; it refers to the Kingdom of God to come as a present-day way of inhabiting our own place and time. The singularity at the end of the sentence belongs to the other, but it is scarcely to be distinguished from my singular otherness to myself.

10. In *Excitable Speech: A Politics of the Performative* (New York: Routledge, 1997), 1–43, Judith Butler speaks of a primary "linguistic vulnerability" that shapes our response to performative utterances; elsewhere she suggests that as subjects we are fundamentally dependent on a power that "subjects" us to the impossible demand of giving an account of ourselves (*Giving an Account of Oneself* [New York: Fordham University Press, 2005]). My formulations here are indebted to her models, from which they nonetheless dissent: in the first case by suggesting that we make as much as we find our susceptibility to performative force, and in the second by diverting the giving of an account from the self to the event of understanding and by regarding demand as only one of the modes by which the accounting may be elicited.

11. Slavoj Žižek, *Interrogating the Real*, ed. Rex Butler and Scott Stephens (London: Continuum, 2006), 241.

12. "Like light, [the imagination] add nothing, except itself." From "The Figure of the Youth as Virile Poet," in Stevens, *The Necessary Angel: Essays on Reality and the Imagination* (New York: Random House, 1965), 61.

13. From "Dichtung und Warheit (An Unwritten Poem)," in W. H. Auden, *Collected Poems*, ed. Edward Mendelssohn (New York: Random House, 1991), 650.

14. Ludwig Wittgenstein, *The Blue and Brown Books: Preliminary Studies for the Philosophical Investigations*, ed. Rush Rhees (New York: Harper and Row, 1965), 166. This work is hereafter cited as *BB*.

15. See Daniel Tiffany, "Lyric Substance: On Riddles, Materialism, and Poetic Obscurity," *Critical Inquiry* 28 (2001): 72–99; and, with specific reference to music, Lawrence Kramer, "Saving the Ordinary: Beethoven's 'Ghost' Trio and the Wheel of History," *Beethoven Forum* 12 (2005): 50–81.

16. Antonio Damasio, *Descartes' Error: Emotion, Reason, and the Human Brain* (New York: Grosset/Putnam, 1994), 173–75. For Damasio, the somatic markers work in "partnership" (p. 175) with more explicit, traditionally higher-order forms of cognition. But a cautionary note is needed on this point: As Ruth Leys ("The Turn to Affect: A Critique," *Critical Inquiry* 37 [2011]: 434–72) has argued, this way of characterizing the process tends to reproduce the Cartesian mind–body dualism that the hypothesis sets out to correct. The inference seems clear: The partnership Damasio envisions is viable only if the difference between the partners is *not* (to continue the reference to Descartes) clear and distinct. Leys's critique extends to an influential school of "affectivist" thought that regards affect as an elemental substratum of sentience immune to comprehension or description; Damasio is included in this group because he supposes that the affects fall into a clear typology of elemental types, a kind of affective semiotics. *Expression* and *truth* can in part be read as an effort that, adopting Leys's refutation of the affectivist position, seeks to formulate the beginnings of an alternative.

17. Judith Butler, "Bodily Inscriptions, Performative Subversions," and "Imitation and Gender Insubordination," in *The Judith Butler Reader*, ed. Sarah Salih with Judith Butler (Oxford: Blackwell, 2004), 90–118, 119–137, respectively. From the latter: "If the 'I' is a site of repetition, that is, if the 'I' only achieves the semblance of identity through a certain repetition itself, then the 'I' is always displaced by the very repetition that sustains it" (125).

18. Nicholas Cook, "Music as Performance," in *The Cultural Study of Music: A Critical Introduction*, ed. Martin Clayton, Trevor Herbert, and Richard Middleton (New York: Routledge, 2002), 208.

19. *The Seminar of Jacques Lacan, Book VII: The Ethics of Psychoanalysis, 1959–60*, ed. Jacques-Alain Miller, and trans. Dennis Potter (New York: Norton, 1992), 105. See also Lawrence Kramer, *Musical Meaning: Toward a Critical History* (Berkeley: University of California Press, 2001), 165–66; and *Opera and Modern Culture: Wagner and Strauss* (Berkeley: University of California Press, 2004), 5–14.

20. *Shelley's Poetry and Prose*, ed. Donald Reiman and Sharon Powers (New York: Norton, 1977), 449.

21. Rainer Maria Rilke, *Sonnets to Orpheus*, trans. M. D. Herter Norton (New York: Norton, 1962), 25. This passage is from Part 1, no. 5, ll. 4–7, 9.

22. Giorgio Agamben, *Language and Death: The Place of Negativity*, trans. Karen E. Pinkus, with Michael Hardt (Minneapolis: University of Minnesota Press, 1991), 31–37.

23. Celan, "Meridian," appendix to Jacques Derrida, *Sovereignties in Question: The Poetics of Paul Celan*, ed. Thomas Dutoit and Outi Passanen (New York: Fordham University Press, 2005), 173–85.

24. "Shibboleth: For Paul Celan," *Sovereignties in Question*, 16–37.

25. "Shibboleth," *Sovereignties in Question*, 37.

26. "Shibboleth," *Sovereignties in Question*, 38.

27. "Shibboleth," *Sovereignties in Question*, 38. In the original: "Cet autre poème qui met en œuvre musicale un indéchiffrable ou un insignifiant (Undeutbares). Il se clôt sur ces mots qui disent si peu, et plus que tout, inoubliables dès lors et faits pour passer inapercus de la mémoire, dans leur intraduisable simplicité, leur simplicité scandée toutefois." *Schibboleth: Pour Paul Celan* (Paris: Galilée, 1986), 69.

28. "Politics and Poetics of Witnessing," *Sovereignties in Question*, 65–96.

29. Wallace Stevens, "An Ordinary Evening in New Haven," xii, *Collected Poems of Wallace Stevens* (New York: Knopf, 1954), 473.

30. Wittgenstein, *Lectures and Conversations on Aesthetics, Psychology, and Religious Belief*, ed. Cyril Barrett (1967; repr. Berkeley: University of California Press, 2007), 29.

31. "The Origin of the Work of Art," 52–55, 60–64.

32. See, for example, Stanley Cavell, *In Quest of the Ordinary: Lines of Skepticism and Romanticism* (Chicago: University of Chicago Press, 1988), esp. Chapter 6, "The Uncanniness of the Ordinary," 153–78. In the first chapter, Cavell observes that "the sense of the ordinary my work derives from the practice of the later Wittgenstein and from J. L. Austin, in their attention to the language of ordinary life, is underwritten by Emerson and Thoreau in their devotion to the thing they call the common, the familiar, the near, the low" (p. 4). To Cavell's emphasis on language, I would add two things: the mutual implication of language and perception, which is fundamental to Wittgenstein's thinking of the "-as" and the aspect, and the recognition that the language of ordinary life is not necessarily, perhaps not even often, "ordinary language."

33. Jacques Ranciére, "The Aesthetic Dimension: Aesthetics, Politics, Knowledge," *Critical Inquiry* 36 (2009): 1–19.

34. *Being and Time*, 225–56.

35. Theodor W. Adorno, *Aesthetic Theory* (1970), ed. and trans. Robert Hullot-Kentor with Rolf Tiedemann and Gretel Adorno (Minneapolis: University of Minnesota Press, 1997), 118–36. As Richard Leppert observes in his annotated edition of Adorno's *Essays on Music* (Berkeley: University of California Press, 2002), "enigmaticalness" was particularly crucial to Adorno's conception of music in the modern era: "The [enigmatic] residue of the uncertain . . . constitutes a resistance to music's instrumental utilization. The enigmatic is music's connection to the unattainable wherein lies utopia" (p. 98).

36. On hermeneutic windows, see Lawrence Kramer, *Music as Cultural Practice: 1800–1900* (Berkeley: University of California Press, 1990), 1–20; on semantic performatives, see Kramer, *Interpreting Music* (Berkeley: University of California Press,) 174–82.

37. Heidegger, "The Thing," *Poetry Language Thought*, 161–84, esp. 165–67; and Lacan, *Ethics of Psychoanalysis*, 120–23.

38. *Remembrance of Things Past*, trans. C. K. Scott Moncrieff and Terence Kilmartin (New York: Vintage, 1982), 228.

39. William C. Carter, *Marcel Proust: A Life* (New Haven: Yale University Press, 2002), 898.

40. Gilles Deleuze and Félix Guattari, *A Thousand Plateaus: Capitalism and Schizophrenia* (1980), trans. Brian Massumi (Minneapolis: University of Minnesota Press, 1987), 167–92.

41. Wittgenstein, *Culture and Value*, ed. G. H. von Wright in collaboration with Heikki Nyman, trans. Peter Winch (Chicago: University of Chicago Press, 1994), 37.

42. Walter Benjamin, "On Some Motifs in Baudelaire," in *Selected Writings, 1938–1940*, trans. Harry Zohn and ed. Michael William Jennings (Cambridge, MA: Harvard University Press, 2003), 311–55.

43. "The Voice of Persephone: Music in Mixed Media," Chapter 8 of *Musical Meaning: Toward a Critical History* (see pp. 182–84).

FOUR

Melodic Speech

EXPRESSION IS ENVOICING.

WHERE DOES SPEECH COME IN? And what does it bring when it comes?
In 1877, Nietzsche wrote a scathing paragraph about words: "In relation to music all communication with words is of the shameless sort; the word dilutes and stultifies; the word depersonalizes; the word makes the uncommon common." One really needs the original German to grasp just how drastically this statement demonstrates the opposite of what it says: "Im Verhältnis zur Musik ist alle Mitteiling durch Worte vom schamlöloser Art; das Wort verdünnt und verdummt; das Wort entpersönlicht; das Wort macht das Ungemeine gemein."[1] The phonetic and rhetorical voicing of these sentences, their accumulating cadences, the underlying murmur of their *m* sounds, their quasi-musical modulation of the very words their words affect to condemn (from *Worte* to *das Wort, das Wort, das Wort;* from *verdünnt* to *verdumm*t; from *das Ungemeine* to *gemein*), the final backflip and compression, again with the echoing *m—**macht das Ungemeine gemein***: Nietzche's utterance gleefully gives itself the lie. It might even be said to do exactly what it claims words can't do: It makes something common—the old canard that music expresses what words cannot—uncommon.

And it does so musically. Its demonstrative point is that it does not communicate with its words but by adding music to them; it mimics expressive speech; it scripts a melody of inflection, accent, emphasis, and tone. Implicit in this verbal performance is a distinction between language, "the word," as a social and conventional form, and language as individual utterance— something much like de Saussure's famous later distinction between *langue* and *parole*. As common property, language for Nietzsche cannot help but depersonalize and thus to make the incomparably singular character of our experience into something "shallow, thin, relatively stupid, general, sign, herd signal."[2] But as music, as an utterance rendered singular by rhythm, intonation, and timbre, the word, Zarathustra-like, overcomes itself: becomes, one might say, the overword.

As Nietzsche himself put it, "One never communicates thoughts: One communicates motions, mimic signs, which then get read back from us into thoughts."[3] More music, mimic signs, phonetic movements: "Man teilt sich nie Gedanken mit: man teilt sich Bewegungen mit, mimische Zeichen, welche von uns auf Gedanken hin zurückgelesen werden." The melody here sounds like something in Wittgenstein's ear, an envoicing of the ordinary at its strangest: The motions and mimic signs just somehow get read back into thoughts—no explanation; they just do. Thought is never experienced as such but only as melodic speech "read back."

What Nietzsche cannot accept is that the melody of thought does not automatically become common just because it is ordinary. Nietzsche loved living on the margins; he does not recognize what Cavell calls the uncanniness of the ordinary[4] or the strange truth, which preoccupied Wittgenstein, that living in the light of that uncanniness, under its changing aspects, is hard work. One has to compose, to musicalize, one's address to the ordinary with the same self-consuming care found in Nietzsche's mimic speech against words.

But what, then, of the extraordinary? There are times when speech melody detaches itself from words and acts on its own; times when expressive vocalization can obliterate language to form a fully melodic speech that gets read back into thought; times when the voice, literal or figurative, speaks, literally or figuratively, *in* melody rather than *with* words. Such speech carries the force of address, Nietzsche's movements and mimic signs, regardless of whether its words are understood. Although the words may provide a point of orientation, they determine nothing. They melt into their phonetic substance and serve primarily as the medium for the melody as the ordinary order of speech turns itself inside out.

Walt Whitman calls this becoming-melody of speech "vocalism" and regards it as the link between the performative power of language and the musical resonance of the body:

All waits for the right voices;
Where is the practis'd and perfect organ? where is the develop'd soul?

For I see every word uttered thence has deeper, sweeter, new sounds,
impossible on less terms.

I see brains and lips closed, tympans and temples unstruck,
Until that comes which has the quality to strike and unclose,
Until that comes which has the quality to bring forth what lies slumbering
forever ready in all words. ("Vocalism," ll. 16–21)[5]

Words from the right voices, practiced in the art of melodic speech, reverse the
ordinary relation of words and sounds; the words carry the sounds, which give
both pleasure and meaning, sweetness and depth, not the sounds the words.

Melodic speech awakens this latent (slumbering) sonorous substance by two
means, striking and unclosing. Striking affects the listener: The vocal melody
strikes the eardrums and strikes up in the pulse at the temples (Whitman's
text, like Nietzsche's, gives mimic signs of this reverberant force with punning
overtones of orchestral sonority and the resonance of sacred spaces). Unclosing affects the speaker: The vocal melody parts the lips and opens the mind,
turning both into gateways through which the awakened sonority issues forth.

Melodic speech is thus the excess of speech melody over its ordinary
powers. It sounds only rarely, because those powers are more than considerable. (Again: the ordinary is not the common.) It is, after all, by my tone that
you can tell whether my words are ironic, whether I am sincere or deceiving
or deceived, whether I am lying, whether I am really listening to you. In all
these cases, tone is the test of the word. But in melodic speech, the word is the
instrument of tone. In melodic speech, tone speaks for itself. The expressive
dimension of voice interrupts itself; instead of acting as what Giorgio Agamben calls a signature, a supplement authorizing a certain force or meaning in
what is said,[6] tone becomes the intelligible substance of utterance. The melody
of melodic speech is at the same time both the expression and the truth.

Jane Campion's film adaptation of Henry James's *The Portrait of a Lady*
(a work I have found instructive before[7]) offers a particularly resonant example of this fusion. Shortly before the end, the heroine, Isabel Archer, keeps a
vigil by the deathbed of her beloved cousin, Ralph Touchett. The two have
long been drawn to one another, but any romantic possibility between them
has been quashed from the outset by Ralph's tuberculosis. It is only as he
nears death that the suppressed eroticism in Isabel's relationship with him
can find its voice.

Or more exactly its melody: for as Isabel virtually croons to him, the power of her utterance, her aria, comes to consist not in what her words say but in the incessant, murmuring, caressing movement of her voice. (James's text creates a similar impression: "She had lost all her shame, all wish to hide things. Now he must know; she wished him to know. . . . 'You did something once—you know it. O Ralph, you've been everything! What have I done for you—what can I do today? I would die if you could live. But I don't wish you to live; I would die myself, not to lose you.' Her voice was as broken as his own, and full of tears and anguish."[8]) The mimic signs of that movement are echoed both by the camera and by the emergence on the soundtrack of music in the style of a late-Romantic piano concerto. The music has its own story to tell, because the soundtrack has previously leaned heavily on extracts from Schubert, especially the devastating (and, in context, obviously allegorical) Quartet in D Minor, "Death and the Maiden." The exchange of this music for a Rachmaninoff sound-alike confirms (supplements, explicates) what Isabel's vocal melody already says: that the erotic consummation always assumed impossible between these two is now taking place, that it is taking place in the speech melody, not figuratively but literally, and that this matters greatly despite being, in the worldly sense, too little and too late. The voice that says all this is not Isabel's as such but a voice that speaks through hers, and speaks to her as much as it speaks for her. It says more than she knows and more than she has the power to say herself.

James is a good source of examples in part because he is constantly aware of the expressive force of melodic speech, especially in his sinuously indirect late style:

> He took it all in as she stood there, speaking in whispers by the balustrades; his vision, or rather his audition, was of the sheer immensity, the grandeur, that rose up immeasurably within this little person. It was a tone, no, not so much as that, but the barest intimation of intimations, that she would stand it, whatever came, that suspended this recognition between them. She had the fortitude and no one should imagine she had not. Certainly he would not; and he hung fire a moment to let her know as much—that there could be no shoal on which her bark would founder. He would know it, always, whenever they should meet; he would hear it in or beneath the infinitesimal shadings of her voice; he would feel it vibrate in the very air between them.

But there is a problem here. Henry James did not write the paragraph just quoted; I did. Personally, I think it sounds just like him, but regardless of that, it obviously *means* to sound just like the Henry James of *The Golden Bowl* or "The Beast in the Jungle," and the very possibility of that intention is something I want to consider more closely than usual.

More closely, because, as usual, we are too used to the usual. (As noted previously, melodic speech itself emerges as a concept when we stand back from the ordinary life of speech melody.) The first thing one would be likely to say about my phantom paragraph is that it is written in the style of James. This is true in a certain obvious sense: the handling of periodic sentences, certain turns of phrase, the type of scene evoked, all might be called Jamesian traits—not traits unique to him, of course, but traits that have so to speak been appropriated to him as personal hallmarks by his standing as a canonical author. These traits would ordinarily be supposed to add up to a characteristic tone, the "voice" of James as an author. Style, as the old saying goes, is the man. But here, too, there is a problem.

The voice is not the simple product of a collection of traits, nor is it something we infer from the presence or absence of such traits. The voice is something we "hear" (that is, imagine hearing) immediately. We do not need to reflect on it; we recognize it. This voice is something we perceive in the way that we ourselves voice, or intone, the Jamesian language in our mind's ear. We have to imagine this voice, and to do that we have to imagine its tonality, its timbre, its pace, its flow, its quality. But we do not imagine it piecemeal; we imagine it whole.

The voice, in short, transcends the traits on which it apparently rests, so that it is always the voice that seems to produce the traits, not the other way around. It is easy to sense this apropos my phantom paragraph. If you read it at first under the (misleading) impression that it was by James, the voice you heard in it was James's. Once the paragraph was revealed as the work of a James impersonator, the voice would be different. Or would it? One might hear it differently on subsequent readings, and one might hear it differently in retrospect, but the original impression could not simply be nullified. The matter of whose voice is there would prove to be not so simple. The voice would belong neither to James nor the impersonator, but to the subject position that makes possible the passage between them. And since James, no less than his impersonator, had to craft that voice, had to find and arrange the words to be intoned and endow them with just the melody one would recognize as Jamesian, the mere fact that the actual Henry James wrote one passage and an imposter the other would not settle the issue of the voice's identity.

The voice in the phantom paragraph might well be James's, no matter who wrote the words. And the voice in certain paragraphs actually written by James might belong to someone else. Anyone might have access to the Jamesian voice (which is not the same as James's voice), the intoning of which might either smother and deaden the participating subject ("smother and deaden" is a phrase lifted from James's *The Wings of the Dove*) or, on the contrary—and there are, one might say in a Jamesian tone, many stations in between, a vast parti-colored array of variations—might induce a sense of mystery and wonder (this phrase is stolen from *The Portrait of a Lady*, from a scene of talk, described but not quoted, between Isabel and Ralph, a scene all of tone, not word).[9] And just whose voice is this?

Let's not answer but lift the parenthesis and go back to the verbal music of the deathbed scene. Unlike the film, the novel stages this scene as a duet. It makes the surge of melody visible—or do I mean audible?—in an abundance of dashes, exclamation points, question marks, repeated words and phrases, and phonetic echoes. For much of the time the normally voluble narrative voice fades into the background, its sinuous line yielding to the compressed speech acts that burst from the mouths of the speakers:

> "Dear Isabel, life is better; for in life there's love. Death is good—but there's no love."
>
> "I never thanked you—I never spoke—I never was what I should be!" Isabel went on. She felt a passionate need to cry out and accuse herself, to let her sorrow possess her. All her troubles, for the moment, became single and melted together in this present pain. "What must you have thought of me? Yet how could I know? I never knew, and I only know to-day because there are people less stupid than I am."
>
> "Don't mind people," said Ralph. "I think I'm glad to leave people."[10]

Unlike the film's concerto-like underscore, the melody of this scene is not an example of late-Romantic effusion; it is the melody of inadequate speech raised to a higher power by the force of its intonation. It is melodic without being eloquent—music stripped bare.

When a melody speaks, it speaks only with the words it has left behind. But when speech becomes melodic, its music is all its own. Even so, melodic speech can combine with actual music; it can assume something of the music's expressive force and perhaps of its contingent identity without, for all that, becoming lost in it. Isabel's "aria" in the film of *The Portrait of a Lady* makes this clear enough, and the source is telling. Melodic speech with a musical underscore is a basic resource of cinematic ecstasy and anguish. In that respect it is an aspect of modernity's dream machine. But what about real life?

The stakes in that question are higher than they appear. Real life, whatever we mean by the term, is too saturated in voice for us to hear it properly. Voice becomes clearer in the semi-silent form of text: semi-silent because in reading text, voice is heard without being spoken or, what amounts to the same thing, spoken in such a way that it cannot, not ever, be heard. To know voice we need to read about it. But what is it that we want to know? What do we need to know?

Recent thinking about voice has passed through two broad phases. The first, associated with Derrida, takes voice as the privileged medium of a presence (of self, consciousness, truth, authority, divinity) that continually slips away from its invocation.[11] There is, to be sure, no escaping voice, but the voice we cannot escape is always escaping us. This becomes mockingly obvious, perhaps, in the face of recent technology, now that the original dream of phonography, the preservation of person through the recording of voice, has morphed into the reality of simulation, the fabrication of person through the programming of voice. We have all become familiar with interactive voice software, which, no matter how "realistic" it sounds, loudly proclaims that the voice we hear is a declaration of absence, not presence. When we talk to that voice, we are talking to no one. It's small comfort that our supposed interlocutor could never pass a Turing test, at least not this week; we'd be better off being fooled.

The second phase, associated with Mladen Dolar and Slavoj Žižek, sees in voice a more fundamental self-division between the (half) light of presence, both coming and going, and the impenetrable darkness of what they call the object-voice: an, or the, unsymbolizable remainder found in every voice, charged with dread, and felt most often as the punitive, unloving, and in a sense nonliving voice of law. ("There is no law," Dolar says, "without the voice.")[12] In the realm of the object-voice, voice in the sense of mystery and wonder is a secondary phenomenon; it is a defense, a prosthesis, a prettification. Melodic speech could only be the most egregious instance of this; and music itself (so they argue) is only a bewitchingly effective defense against what is unbearable in the sound of the object-voice. All music is the music of the sirens. Voice, music's double, is a veil over the ugliness of the Real, thinner and more diaphanous than we suppose, and subject to rending at any moment.

But there is nothing that says the remainder must be ugly. That it may be so goes without saying: The voice that smothers and deadens cannot be wished away. But neither can that voice that induces mystery and wonder, which has no less a claim on primacy than its dark double. Where the object-voice bespeaks a primordial deprivation, the void of the inarticulate in the form of a grating noise, what I will call expressive voice bespeaks a primary endowment, the source of the articulate in the form of the audible. Expressive voice is ground of the truthfulness that, as Derrida notes, is the condition of possibility of speech between one person and another;[13] its existence is the reason that tone can communicate in excess of words. The two forms in which we hear this best are speaking melody and melodic speech.

Both speaking melody and melodic speech are products of the uneasy, never completed fusion of speech with voice.

Speaking melody substitutes speech for voice so that what is spoken is known even though it is not heard. If voice represents presence or origin or their promise or lure across a distance, speaking melody insists on the loss of voice in the persistence of speech, the nullification of the uniqueness of voice in the iterability of the word. Speaking melody carries distance into presence. If voice represents the material remainder of law or the traumatic Real, speaking melody insists on the power of the other Lacanian registers, the imaginary of the unheard voice and the symbolic of verbal memory, to keep the Real at bay, to limit its claims. Speaking melody keeps presence at a distance.

Melodic speech subordinates speech to voice so that what is voiced is known regardless of what is spoken. Speech melody is everywhere, but it is not *heard* everywhere. For speech melody to be heard as such the word must go not unheard but unheeded, either in vocal arias in which speaking as such, not the thing spoken, is the expressive performance (Isabel to Ralph), or in vocal music in the state of songfulness, where singing is heard so intently that the words sung cease to matter, even if we still understand them.[14] If voice represents presence or origin or their promise or lure across a distance, melodic speech insists on the loss of the word in the event of voice, the nullification of the iterability of the word in the uniqueness of voice. If voice represents the material remainder of law or the traumatic Real, melodic speech, insofar as it is melodic, insists on an alternative for which the Lacanian registers have no place, in hearing of which law is suspended and opacity loses the power to traumatize.

But here a contradiction arises with no counterpart elsewhere. For insofar as the excess of voice over speech is *not* melodic, not subject to being heard as (a) music, the force of the traumatic Real is redoubled; it blares, becomes cruel and aggressive, drowns out the subjectivity of the listener. For this, perhaps, the only remedy (if not a cure) is the re-melodization of voice.

All of these possibilities represent the fragility of the tie between voice and speech, a tie that ordinarily holds in everyday life (or we seek to act as if it did) but that can always, at any moment, fray, loosen, or break, sometimes for the better and sometimes—not.

Music can imitate speech melody without the involvement of voice. Rousseau, indeed, thought that melody as such originated in the imitation of speech sounds and should never stray too far from its origin. But he said so precisely because he thought it had strayed too far already. Instrumental melody may or may not have emerged from, or as, vocal mimesis, but it is not mimetic as such, and when it becomes so for expressive reasons its favored object is song (it becomes cantabile). The musical imitation of speech melody is an exceptional event, just as the overwhelming of actual utterance by its own speech melody is an exceptional event. And it is a historically belated event, apparently one of the consequences of the European Enlightenment, perhaps precisely as a resistance to too much enlightenment, the mark of a desire to retain a degree of enchantment by giving what is most singular and least explicable in the voice a chance to be heard as such. The "as such" requires a certain framing, a certain aesthetic distance, which is why the mimesis of speech melody rather than speech melody itself becomes the most highly charged object. Distance thus becomes basic to the aesthetics of musical melodic speech, albeit in direct and contradictory combination with a sense of exceptional intimacy and proximity.

Perhaps the earliest example occurs in the first movement of Beethoven's "Tempest" Sonata (the Piano Sonata no. 17, op. 31, no. 2, composed 1802), where a voice ventriloquized by the piano interrupts the turbulent course of the music. Suddenly, inexplicably, we are listening to a recitative—even straining to hear it, for it comes sotto voce. The voice assumes its common humanity by sounding (and sounding again; the repetition is both uncanny and confirmatory) as a plea across a distance: not as a plea for anything in particular, but as the vocal melody of pleading that can seek only the recognition and sympathy to which its identity is addressed. This episode marks a double break. It is equally an aesthetic rupture and a rupture of the aesthetic. It is based on the style of vocal rather than instrumental recitative; it is a genuine mimesis rather than a generic allusion. And its mimesis resonates. As music this voice does not come out of nowhere. It comes from the place of a mysterious arpeggio that begins the movement and twice returns to open the voice's auditory vista. But only its returns link the static arpeggio to the potentiality of voice, call, and appeal. As mimesis the voice comes precisely out of nowhere, out of an indiscernibly distant recess that its utterance converts into a somewhere, a primary locus of human self-definition, the place of an oracular inwardness folding itself outward.[15]

Certain earlier works anticipate this moment of breakthrough. There is the slow movement of J. S. Bach's Violin Concerto in E, BWV 1042 (1717): a long, unbroken arc of mournful violin melody introduced by a ritornello in the style of a recitative that, before its framing return at the end, is repeatedly sublimated by the soloist's cantabile. There is the slow movement of Haydn's String Quartet op. 55, no. 2 (1788), where, however, pleading speech evolves into lamenting instrumental song, recitative to arioso. And there is the slow movement of Mozart's Piano Concerto no. 9, K. 271 (1775), where passages of instrumental recitative for first violins hold the anticipatory place of a voice to come. The emergence of that voice anchors the pathos of the movement in the piano's own quasi-human voice, something far from established at this early moment in the instrument's history. (Is it an accident that all four of these examples are slow movements that trace voice to a moment of suffering, perhaps to the pressure of need that contemporary theories held responsible for the origin of language?) The voice is one that the piano gradually comes to try out, share, and, at the very end of the movement, to take as its own.

Or take the slow movement of Mozart's *Sinfonia Concertante* for Violin and Viola, K. 374 (1779), another venture in melancholy sensibility. Here the effect of melodic speech passes, James-like (or, more properly, opera-like), back and forth between the two soloists. Violin and viola take the orchestra's mournful utterance as an invitation for dialogue not with the orchestra but with each other, and consolingly so. Their dialogue becomes an intimate exchange, an emotional intermingling, as their voices, distinct but closely akin, turn the ruling convention—that each soloist has a turn at the thematic material—into something motivated and internalized. The orchestra, meanwhile, resigns its usual role of representing the social body and becomes an acoustic matrix, a kind of sonorous body of potential feeling, the threshold between sound as substance and sound as meaning.[16]

This small genealogy of canonical works may be taken as the armature of a symbolic history, that is, of a symbolic arrangement whose force has some degree of operation in the present and helps to establish a frame of reference in which other examples may be heard. Notable among the latter is the penultimate number of Schumann's piano cycle *Davidsbündlertänze*, op. 6 (1837), marked "Wie aus der Ferne" (As from the Distance). This is a piece in which the melody imitating melodic speech hovers just over or sinks into the midst of a densely but transparently multilayered pianistic texture. As it comes and goes, the distant voice becomes the voice of distance itself. Hearing it as voice becomes a reflection on the act of hearing afar, of hearing-for, of trying to hearken. Just for this reason, perhaps, the work as a whole cannot end with the vocal mimesis, which eludes closure by its very definition. *Davidsbündlertänze* ends instead with an off-kilter (rarefied, dissociated) dance. But another of Schumann's piano cycles very nearly does end with a fiction of melodic speech. We will return to "Wie aus der Ferne," a piece that drew Wittgenstein's close attention, in Chapter 5. For the present, there is something to learn from that other instance which does almost speak its way to a close. The title of the piece involved virtually promises as much; the piece is "Der Dichter Spricht" (The Poet Speaks), the closing number of Schumann's *Kinderszenen* (Scenes of Childhood, 1838; see Example 4.1). The poet's voice is presumably retrospective, perhaps nostalgic, perhaps a little elegiac. What else can we hear in it?

This voice too is an interruption. It arises as an unmeasured passage between two statements of a simple, tranquil, block-chord melody that lapses, as if unwittingly, or with the presumed innocence of childhood, into mystery. The mystery appears as a veil of arcane harmony that enwraps the second half of the melody and leads it to a cadence in the wrong key. A brief attempt to turn back only leads further away, to an even more remote tonal space from which, after a silence, the melodic speech of the poet emerges. Starting from, and dipping into, the registral space of the music around it, the voice traces a sinuous ascending path into a region entirely its own, lingering at each stage of its progress. And then it disappears.

Unlike the voices in our other examples, this one is neither a call from afar nor an echo of opera. It is a personal murmur, and the distance it invokes is not external. This is an interiorized voice, perhaps talking only to itself, perhaps even subvocally. Its emergence perhaps marks a historical shift in the conception of voice in which the art of speech, derived from classical rhetoric, gives way to the nature of unmediated self-expression. In 1833,

EXAMPLE 4.1 Robert Schumann, "Der Dichter Spricht" from *Kinderszenen* (complete).

John Stuart Mill famously registered this shift with the maxim that "Eloquence is heard; poetry is overheard."[17] (Mill applied the same distinction to music; he thought that Mozart and Beethoven, though experts at musical oratory, had discovered how to give music a poetic voice.) The voice in which the "poet" of *Kinderszenen* speaks is overhead across the unmeasurable—and immeasurable—distance of its own singularity, remote even from itself. The poet's own voice, which has no owner, would be mute except for that distance. It is equally remote from both past and present; it withdraws itself ironically in the very act of coming forth as speech; it absorbs itself and those who overhear it in the meshes of pure vocality where meaning, we would like to think, is distilled to its expressive essence.

As Mill tells and James shows us, speech alone can do what this melody does. As Schumann both shows and tells, melody alone can address us with the force of speech. It is never a simple matter of either getting past the other. We don't know what Schumann's poet says, but we do know the kind of thing he might have said: something fantastic, something frightening, something enchanting—something that might allow the modern adult, who, sadly, knows better, to regain a sense of wonder.

High stakes for such simple music. But they can get much higher.

Speaking melody normally comes about when speech is subtracted from song, leaving a residue of voice in a music otherwise rendered voiceless. But melodic speech can sometimes precede a speaking melody that it then becomes. The music comes about by transcribing a speech melody that has already been inscribed with the traces of a speech act that then finds its expression but not its enunciation in the music.

Steve Reich's musical essay in Holocaust remembrance, *Different Trains* (1988), identifies this expressive transcription with the formation of historical memory. Reich recorded the voices of three Holocaust survivors and of two figures from his own childhood in the period between 1939 and 1941, when as a child he traveled frequently by train between New York and Los Angeles and when, as he realized looking back, "if I had been in Europe during this period, as a Jew I would have had to ride very different trains." The bridge between past and present is the melodic transcription of the recorded voices, to which Reich assigned specific pitches and rhythms in standard musical notation. Insofar as the music (for strings, with recordings of train whistles added) composes itself of these speaking melodies, *Different Trains* does not "set" its voices but is quite literally called into being by them. In this music, the past speaks—musically—without ever having sung, a transformation on which Reich reflects ironically by closing the work with a reminiscence of a girl's being made to sing, in one of the camps, for the Germans.

Different Trains often juxtaposes its speaking melody closely with the recorded voices from which the melody derives. The result is strange, uncanny even: We hear the speaking voices as if they were singing, and though we know they are not, and can *hear* they are not, we nonetheless yield to a second, simultaneous, phantom impression that these voices have broken into (have been broken into) song. So the past, in which singing was lost even when, as with the girl in the camp, it was found, after all does sing, in the act of speaking.

In context, the link between speaking melody and loss, the equivocation between memory as recalling, a re-calling, calling back, and memory as division and mourning, becomes closer than ever. The crux of this process comes in the third and last movement, when the voice of Lawrence Davies, a Pullman porter, says, "But today, they're all gone." He is referring to the fast coast-to-coast trains of the period, but the reference begins to break loose from its mooring even as he, that is, his voice, says it. Meanwhile the music has already begun to echo and amplify the statement in the speaking melody transcribed from Davies's melodic speech. As it does, his statement, "they're all gone," as heard without speech in the music "thrown" by his voice, becomes a sober recognition of the endless train of the dead whose absence forms the unspoken context and reproach for the voices of the then-living that, in principle, can (unlike the voices of those others) still have acoustic life even after they too become the voices of the dead.[18]

A series of important modern thinkers including Freud, Heidegger, Levinas, and Derrida link the genesis of responsibility, the essential correlate of a free self capable of decision and action in its own name, to the experience of a call, the condition of being addressed by another. One becomes responsible by answering the call, by showing oneself able to make a response, to be response/able. And one answers the call without appropriating it, by opening oneself to whatever and whoever issues the call, by acknowledging that one owes this call an answer.

For Heidegger the experience of the call is primordial, independent of any actual address, utterance, speech, or expressive form. He puts this by saying that

Dasein, human being, calls to itself, but *not* in a relationship of identity or self-reflection. On the contrary: "'It' calls, against our expectations and even against our will.... The call comes *from* me and yet from *beyond* me."[19] The call comes from me but "I" do not call; rather I am called on. The call comes from me but it does not belong to me—if anything, I belong to it, I am indebted to or guilty before it, I am *schuldig*, the German word for both "guilty" and "indebted" that may also mean "responsible (for)."[20] (The usual word for "responsible," *verant-wortlich*, would translate literally as "answerable," the English term that also links responsibility to the obligation to respond, to answer whatever call falls upon one.) For Freud, the call comes from the Oedipal father, whom we may tease apart (somewhat in Heidegger's manner) from any particular person and recast as the Lacanian name-of-the-father, the place of paternal authority in the symbolic order, the big Other. Whereas Heidegger's call stems from within but comes from without, Freud's call stems from without but comes from within. For Levinas, the call comes from the mortality of others as inscribed in and uttered from the human face, which in its otherness is also the face, one of the faces, of God.[21] For Derrida, the call comes from any and all of these places. It comes, so to speak, from the place God would have if God had a place, from the locus of the unthought and unuttered that demands of the responsible person a continual effort of thought and utterance.[22]

Left unanswered and indeed unasked in this series of conceptions is a question that the concept of melodic speech brings to mind immediately: Does the call to responsibility address us as voice or as speech? The voice exceeds what it utters, but every utterance exceeds the voice that speaks it. Do we hold ourselves answerable to the infinitely reiterable utterance or to the singular material substance of the other who utters it? A Wittgensteinian answer would make itself responsible to a language game. Our language suggests the priority of voice; we speak not only of a call but also of a calling, a vocation, an invocation, evocation, a voicing, the vocative. The notion of response, responsiveness, of answerability, carries the same suggestion: One voice calls to another, one voice answers another.

But we might also divide the call with reference to its effects. If the call comes as speech it comes as law, perhaps as accusation or remonstrance, inextricable from its determinate content, its doctrine or commandment. If the call comes as voice it comes (as Derrida seeks to argue) as a gift: an offer and a proof of one's own singularity and therefore a mandate to assume the free subjectivity that, without such a call and its free and open answer, would be an illusion at best.

These alternatives are not evenly balanced. By Derrida's account, the call as speech leaves one unfree and nonresponsible because it preempts its own response; it leaves us unresponsive. Simply to follow the law, to do as one is told, is to act as a device, not as subject: "If decision-making is relegated to a knowledge that it is content to follow or develop, it is no more a responsible decision, it is the technical deployment of a cognitive apparatus, the simple mechanistic deployment of a theorem."[23] To be sure, a responsible decision must somehow be an informed decision. There is no avoiding the contradiction implicit in this necessity. But for all that the decision must, to be responsible, exceed any and every knowledge that informs it; it must decide what cannot be decided. Responsibility begins by assuming responsibility for itself. Its decisions must be made "independently of knowledge; that will be the condition of a practical idea of freedom."[24] Only a call without law, beyond the law, a call and a voice without content, can offer the possibility of a genuine response, a responsible answer, and therefore a medium in which a singular subjectivity can act and be.

The call then comes first as voice, not as speech, even if it comes in speech. And it leaves us with a certain demand that is both cognitive and ethical. This demand forms one of the crossroads of expression and truth. One, but it is one that is met with everywhere.

In what sense can this expression be true?

The response to expression, the meeting of one expression by another, is a microcosm of this overarching condition. Behind whatever particulars, perhaps minute particulars, may be at stake in the response to expression, there stretches the horizon of the broader stakes put forth by the call. As I suggest elsewhere with specific reference to one of the thinkers on call here:

> [For Levinas], who broaches the question in the sphere of ethics, the responsibility both to feel and to understand arises in the demand that I respond to, be responsive to and therefore responsible for, the call that reaches me from someone else, the Other in a positive, not a stigmatized sense.[25] I fail to answer this call if I do no more than repeat it. Only by venturing forth with an answer that carries both myself and the call into the hermeneutic circle do I do any justice at all to the human connection sought in the encounter. . . . Levinas is concerned with human suffering, and the stakes in the responsibility he describes are far higher than anything posed by our encounters with musical works—as long as those encounters take place in open societies where aesthetic immersion is never a political crime. But works are, after all,

composed by people, and our response to them, our response-ability, does count for something in human terms. So the same link that Levinas finds between the ethical and the cognitive does apply, though with lesser urgency, to the encounter with musical and other works of art.[26]

This kind of response, however, as the effort to answer implies, takes the form of speech. It seems as if we answer the call as voice with response as speech. If we want to answer more fully, to answer as we are and with everything we are, so that, as Wallace Stevens once put it, we find a place "Beneath the rhapsodies of fire and fire,/Where the voice that is in us makes a true response,/Where the voice that is great within us rises up" ("Evening without Angels")[27], we must somehow find our way back from speech to voice. And we must do so responsibly: not by empty peals of vocalization (a kind of ex-vocation) but by finding the path by which speech is peeled away to reveal the voice behind it. It is at the end of that path that we encounter melodic speech.

There is a certain parallel here to the relation between the words and the melody of a song. Wittgenstein invokes that relation as a metaphor for what does *not* happen between saying something and thinking it: "If [speaking and thinking] stood in the relation of the words and the melody of a song, we could leave out the speaking and do the thinking just as we can sing the tune without the words" (*BB,* 42).[28] But this time Wittgenstein has things backward. We might suggest that it is actually quite easy to think or mean something without speaking it as long as the thought or something like it has once been spoken; it is as if each expression left an indelible impression, a trace by which to retrace its path. A gesture, a nod, a glance, a look on the face (even if no one sees it) can then mark the place of the thought once thought, a thought that remains fully articulate even though it is not articulated. But the more important point is the one we learn from the experience of speaking melody. We may be able to sing the tune without uttering the words, but we can rarely sing it *without* the words, the traces of which not only linger in every performance but may at times even be more powerful when they are known without being heard.

We can, however, hear the words and be indifferent to them. We can become indifferent to them because the unfolding of the song circumvents them or peels them away to produce the effect of songfulness that hollows out the words and that here stands as the musical version, the musical imitation, of melodic speech. Perhaps this will happen for a whole song, a whole aria; perhaps it will happen only for a moment. Whatever its duration, its occurrence is the occasion of our response in kind, a response that precisely thinks its answer without yet saying what it is. We all know what this feels like. The song just gets to us. It touches us and imparts a truth by what it expresses.

Perhaps our response will be a silent opening up to the voice that pierces or suffuses us; perhaps the response will be a subvocal cry of our own, or even a voiced one as we sing along while we listen or sing aloud afterward. The voice that calls us qua voice bears the traces of the speech it pares away and, more, calls us just insofar it does so. If the traces disappear entirely, the voice loses its power to call, just as, if the traces appear too fully, the call regresses in the direction of the law. And precisely because the peeling away of speech from voice is also the preservation of the traces of speech in voice, we can be responsible for our response and also give an account of it. We can speak of it in terms that let the tone of our own voice sound through. We can express both the truth of our response and the truth that our response sounds out, the truth that it makes in making it manifest.

What makes a melody expressive? Not its supposedly intrinsic properties, which, like words, do not generate the expressive force they may carry in certain combinations: "All is ripeness" is not "Ripeness is all." There is always a gap separating the semiotic and the semantic, a space of unpredictability, contingency, and chance at the very core of the intelligible. As Giorgio Agamben notes, the recognition of this gap forced itself on the linguist Emile Benveniste in the twilight of the latter's life and career. Benveniste speaks of the gap in almost elegiac tones ("The world of the sign is, in truth, closed. From the sign to the sentence there is no transition"), though he still, Agamben says, sought for a way to bridge it.[29] But it cannot be bridged. The gap can only be leaped, exactly like the larger gap that it portends, the divide between works (discourses, utterances, compositions in every sense of the term) and meanings that, as I have argued elsewhere, is fundamental, radical, and the condition of possibility of interpretation.[30] Melody does not become expressive in being what it is; it becomes what it is in being expressive. And it becomes expressive when we grasp it as making apparent some feature of an occasion, some part of a world, in which we participate with substantial concern. The same principle holds good for expression in general.

These fecund gaps disclose that melody does not become expressive on the basis of codes or conventions; no semiotic framework is rich enough for that. We may and often do find conventional cues helpful, though they are not absolutely necessary; when we listen to melodies with certain traits we know immediately that they are, say, lively or solemn in a general way. But we know nothing about the provenance or particularity of that liveliness or solemnity. Until we do, we do not know what the melody expresses or if it expresses anything at all. Expression arises only where the semiotic has been exceeded, the gap between signs and meanings leaped. What the leap leaves behind is signification, semiotic value; melody becomes expressive when it ceases (or declines) to stand for a generic state of mind but instead acts as an extension of the concern from which a particular state of mind may emerge. The melody becomes expressive not by conveying a content but by assuming an aspect—or a mobile play of aspects, a kind of face.

The expressivity of a melody arises amid its movement around a semantic loop. The most explicit form of this looping occurs when music is applied to verbal and/or visual forms—the text of a song, dramatic speech or action, moving images. As I suggest in *Musical Meaning*, the music in these cases borrows a certain semantic orientation from its address to the imagetext (the network of texts and images that traditionally defines the field of representation in Western culture) and returns what it borrows in enhanced, often changed, ironic, or dissonant form.[31] But this looping actually happens all the time, *whether or not* a particular text or image, description or depiction, is involved. The loop in either case is imaginary, its course sometimes initiated by the generic qualities it needs to surpass, and more often perhaps by other affiliations to nearby semantic fields: cultural and musical allusiveness, historical lore, semantically rich sensory traits, patterns of trope and performativity—the list goes on. Melodies acquire, keep, or lose their expressive force to the extent we circumscribe an occasion of concern with them, much as, in Lacan's account, drives—which I take here as the fundamental form of forces of concern—seek not to extinguish themselves in their object but to circulate endlessly around it.

The formal features of a melody cannot account for these vicissitudes any more than codes and conventions can. Of two equally well-made melodies, one may become an expressive paragon and the other lie inert (a fate that history can reverse as well as mete out). True, it is usually possible to refer expressive force *back onto* formal features, but the phrasing of this acknowledgment is the whole point. The reference, which impels further motion around the semantic loop, comes only *after* the melody has been grasped as an extension of concern. In keeping with the principle of the leap, this grasp is not taken from the melody but brought to it via a semantic detour through the nexus of possibilities that culture, history, and the recipient's capacity for invention make available. What is expressive about the melody is not a group of traits intrinsic to it but the ensemble of traits imparted to it by the movement of concern.

The expression consists in the action of imparting in the form of a making apparent or bringing forth. Concern appears when the melody takes on a vivid new aspect. This statement has to be understood in a strong sense. When expression changes something, what changes is not *an* aspect—not this trait or that. What changes is *aspect*. The whole thing changes. Sometimes everything changes. Expression is the agency of aspect change. It is aspect change as action.

But what action? What change?

Any expressive form either exhibits a generic character or conspicuously lacks one. ("Form," here and throughout, designates a dynamic agency, not a fixed condition.) The first case is by far the more common. But as I have been insisting, generic identity is not expressive; it is classificatory. The would-be expressive form does not arrive at the level of expressiveness until what is generic about it has changed aspect in the direction of the distinctive or, better, of the truly singular. Expressiveness consists in this movement, which is good for only one occasion and on others would have to be renewed or revised or replaced. It occurs neither "in" the expressive form nor "in" the observer but through the unscripted and unrepeatable meeting of the two. The event of expression puts the observer in the position of someone addressed and expects a reply. The implications of this interlocutory mode will concern us in Chapter 5. In the less common case where the expressive form is opaque, the observer has to decide whether to yield to its singularity without demanding intelligibility or to nudge the singular (just) far enough in the direction of the generic to rejoin the expressive agency of making apparent.

The last piece in Schumann's *Davidsbundlertänze*, briefly mentioned earlier, epitomizes the process. The music comes after the work as a whole seems to have ended—emphatically. In an epigraph to the first edition, Schumann called it both "superfluous" and "blissful." It is also repetitive, almost hypnotic (especially if one plays it), and in no hurry to get anywhere. One way to be addressed by it is to absorb oneself with all that and to open oneself up without questioning further to the little squibs of sensuous, almost erotic dissonance that recur throughout the piece with no apparent reason for being except sheer pleasure. Another way is to supply a bit of Wittgensteinian advice—the generic nudge: "Tell yourself it's a *waltz* and you will hear it correctly" (*BB*, 167). Only in this case, what one has to tell oneself is that it is only the ghost of a waltz, a waltz dissolved into shimmering fragments that drift from register to register, hover, linger, and finally drift away into the lowest depths of the bass. The music is the memory of a memory, a fugitive moment that lives on by bidding farewell to itself.

Melody is our culture's paradigmatic instance of indescribable expressiveness—that is, of the inexpressible. In the post-Enlightenment world, precisely this inexpressibility becomes conflated with expression itself.

"There is no expression without a subject." So writes Theodor Adorno,[32] and given his habits of mind he would perhaps be neither surprised nor upset to be told he had gotten things backward. Expression can be faked or mimicked and would not be expression otherwise. The subject from whom it comes is not the subject from whom it feigns to come. Expression can be camouflage. Expression can hover over action in the form of gestures or utterances that can be assumed by any passing subject. There is a great deal of expression without a subject.

It would be much more to the point to say that there is no subject without expression. Subjectivity cannot occur outside the nexus of voice and speech. The voice, the utterance of the body as subject, must be able to transform itself into speech and through speech, the utterance of the person as subject.[33] The reverse must be equally possible. Expression is neither the ground of such transformation nor its outcome; it *is* the transformation. Expressionless speech negates or inhibits subjectivity. Heard from behind a screen, a totally neutral voice would never pass a Turing test as human. Vocal monotony projects automatism. Subjectivity exists only where the world has churned up the waves of voice. Expression is a map of the world, but a map that can only be sensed, not seen.

The subjectivity of everyday life arises amid a continuous hum and rustle of expression. But it is the fate of this expression to rinse away like water off a peaked roof. What is most immediate about expression is self-obliterating; the subjectivity it supports is dim and indefinite. Only in the possibility of its reiteration does expressiveness assume the power of individuation. Casual immediacy is unique without being singular. Only by relinquishing its uniqueness in favor of a reiterable identity can a form of expression rise to the level of singularity that is also the plane of the subject. Only by finding the place of utterance (speech, gesture, the look of the face, the mode of motion) susceptible to repetition, with difference, by oneself or by any self, does the living creature become a human subject.

We become subjects the way tuneless vocalizing becomes a melody. And that last statement—try hearing me voice it, will you? catch the tone secreted in the text—is not a metaphor. Another not-a-metaphor. At times we positively sing ourselves into existence.

LW: If you heard sentences spoken in a monotone, you might be tempted to say that the words were all enshrouded in a particular atmosphere. But wouldn't it be using a peculiar way of representation to say that speaking the sentence in a monotone was adding something to the mere saying of it? Couldn't we even conceive speaking in a monotone as the result of *taking away* from the sentence its inflection? (*BB*, 178.)

LK: This is not just any example; it says something fundamental about saying something. Sentences might be spoken in a monotone in many situations, but in all of them the effect would be one of subtraction. We could even conceive of it as depletion: Monotones make words hollow. Speaking in a monotone is not speaking, properly speaking. No wonder, then, that your metaphor involves a shrouding. Monotone is dead speech.

LW (in a monotone): Because it expresses nothing. But if I speak in a monotone it is not nothing I am expressing. It is the difference between myself and no self. It is an infinitesimal, a minimal distance. I am the not of not-nothing, if nothing else.

LK: Or else you can't speak in a monotone at all. Some intonation will always seep through like a droplet falling on your cheek. All speech insists on its own life, if only for one breath.

LW: Only can you even say so? Whereof one cannot speak one must be silent!

LK: Tone speaks even when words fail; words cannot speak when tone fails. Monotone is no tone. Silence, lived silence, is tone that is gone and tone that is to come. Silence is expressive; between living speakers it is not the opposite of speech.

LW:

NOTES

1. Friedrich Nietzsche, *Der Wille zur Macht* (The Will to Power), v. 10, *Werke: Taschenausgabe* (Leipzig: C. G. Naumann, 1906), no. 810, p. 66.

2. Nietzsche, *The Gay Science*, trans. Walter Kaufmann (New York: Random House, 1974), no. 354, 299–300.

3. *Der Wille zur Macht*, no. 809, p. 66.

4. Stanley Cavell, *In Quest of the Ordinary: Lines of Skepticism and Romanticism* (Chicago: University of Chicago Press, 1988), 153–78.

5. Text from Walt Whitman, *Leaves of Grass*, ed. Sculley Bradley and Harold W. Blodgett (New York: Norton, 1973), 384.

6. Giorgio Agamben, *The Signature of All Things*, trans. Luca D'Isanto with Kevin Attell (Cambridge, New York: Zone 2009).

7. In *Musical Meaning: Toward a Critical History* (Berkeley: University of California Press, 2001), 154–55; and "Recognizing Schubert: Musical Subjectivity and Cultural Change in Jane Campion's *The Portrait of a Lady*," *Critical Inquiry* 28 (2002), 25–52, repr. in Kramer, *Critical Musicology and the Responsibility of Response: Selected Essays* (Aldershot: Ashgate 2006), 209–36.

8. Henry James, *The Portrait of a Lady* (Boston: Houghton Mifflin, 1963), 469. The text is that of the 1908 New York, a revision of the original publication of 1881.

9. James, *The Wings of the Dove* (New York: Digireads.com, 2007), 283; and *Portrait of a Lady*, 357.

10. *Portrait of a Lady*, 470.

11. Derrida, *Of Grammatology*, trans. Gayatri Chakravorty Spivak (Baltimore: Johns Hopkins, 1976), 1–65.

12. Slavoj Žižek, "'I Hear You with My Eyes,' or, The Invisible Master," and Mladen Dolar, "The Object Voice," in Slavoj Žižek and Renata Salacl, ed. *Gaze and Voice as Love Objects* (Durham: Duke University Press, 1996), 90–128 and 7–31, respectively; and Dolar, *A Voice and Nothing More* (Cambridge, MA: MIT Press, 2006). The quotation from Dolar is on p. 102.

13. Derrida, "Typewriter Ribbon," in *Without Alibi*, ed. and trans. Peggy Kamuf (Stanford: Stanford University Press, 2002), 111–12.

14. On songfulness, see Kramer, *Musical Meaning: Toward a Critical History* (Berkeley: University of California Press, 2001), 51–67.

15. For a fuller account, see Kramer, "Primitive Encounters: Beethoven's 'Tempest' Sonata, Musical Meaning, and Enlightenment Anthropology," *Beethoven Forum* 6, ed. Glenn Stanley (Lincoln, Nebraska: University of Nebraska Press, 1998), 31–66, repr. in *Critical Musicology and the Responsibility of Response: Selected Essays* (Aldershot: Ashgate, 2006), 109–44.

16. On the character of this threshold, see Giorgio Agamben, *Language and Death: The Place of Negativity*, trans. Karen E. Pinkus, with Michael Hardt (Minneapolis: University of Minnesota Press, 1991), 31–37.

17. John Stuart Mill, "What is Poetry," in *Early Essays* (London: George Bell, 1897), 208 (accessed via Google Books).

18. For more detailed accounts of *Different Trains,* see Amy Lynn Wlodarski, "The Testimonial Aesthetics of *Different Trains*," *Journal of the American Musicological Society* 63 (2010): 99–147; and Naomi Cumming, "The Horrors of Identification: Reich's *Different Trains*," *Perspectives of New Music* 35 (1997): 129–52. I discuss the work briefly in *Musical Meaning*, 186–87, 280–81.

19. Martin Heidegger, *Being and Time*, trans. John Macquarrie and Edward Robinson (Oxford: Blackwell, 1962), 320.

20. *Being and Time*, 325–35.

21. See Emmanuel Levinas, *Totality and Infinity: An Essay on Exteriority* (1961), trans. Alphonso Lingis (Dordrecht: Kluwer, 1991), 187–253.

22. See Derrida, *The Gift of Death*, trans. David Willis (Chicago: University of Chicago Press, 1995), esp. 82–115.

23. *The Gift of Death*, 24.

24. *The Gift of Death*, 26.

25. Emmanuel Levinas, "The I and the Totality" (1954), in *Entre Nous: Thinking-of-the-Other*, trans. Michael B. Smith and Barbara Harshav (New York: Columbia University Press, 1998), 13–38, esp. 25–27, 30–35.

26. Introduction to *Critical Musicology and the Responsibility of Response*, xiv.

27. *Collected Poems of Wallace Stevens* (New York: Knopf, 1954), 138.

28. Wittgenstein actually wrote "thinking and speaking" but the logic of the statement is clearer if the terms are reversed.

29. *The Signature of All Things*, 60–61.

30. *Musical Meaning: Toward a Critical History* (Berkeley: University of California Press, 2001), 145–63; and *Interpreting Music* (Berkeley: University of California Press, 2010), 1–19.

31. *Musical Meaning*, 163–75.

32. Theodor W. Adorno, *Aesthetic Theory* (1970), ed. and trans. Robert Hullot-Kentor, with Rolf Tiedemann and Gretel Adorno (Minneapolis: University of Minnesota Press, 1997), 52.

33. This is as true of signing as it is of vocalization; the hands of the deaf subject speaking in signs move with their own "voice."

FIVE

Wittgenstein, Music, and the Tone of Crystal

EXPRESSION IS REPLY.

WHAT DO WE DO when we hear music express something?

This question should sound a little strange. It is not the all-too-familiar question, "What does music express?" It is not the related question, "How do we hear what music expresses?" It is a question about the performance of an act, and an act of a particular kind—not a simple recognition but a determination, an act that provides the condition of possibility for the expression we hear. Perhaps we should pose the question in the style of J. L. Austen: What do we do *in hearing* music express something? Asked this way, the question entails a rejection of those other, more traditional questions for asking the wrong things. What music expresses and how we hear it depend on what we *do* in, with, or through a certain hearing. So *that* is what we should be asking about: a practice or habitus, not a type of content or a means of reception. The *what* of musical expression is not a signified and its *how* is not a technique. Each is a force and a participant in a continuous activity with no fixed character.

At the same time, the question *What do we do in hearing music express something?* anticipates part of its own answer. The phrasing of the question implies that hearing music express something is a genre of speech act. It is the auditory equivalent of performative utterances like those that make promises or give consent or seal relationships. This too should sound a little strange. What kind of speech act can I perform without speaking? And how can hearing be an action in the first place? Hearing is not listening; hearing is not something we do but something that happens. But is it really? And why *not* imagine a speech act that occurs mutely, or diverts or defers its utterance?

The answers to the last two questions are, respectively, *not exactly* and *no reason at all*. I may sometimes make a deliberate decision to listen to something I hear, as if to make the passive sense of hearing into something active. But more often, in hearing something, I will find that I have *been* listening to it. I will find myself in the midst of a listening that started I don't know when, perhaps even before I heard a sound. I may equally often think that I'm listening to something only to discover in mid course that I have not really been *hearing* it, that to hear I have to stop what I thought of as listening and listen another way. With music, such moments of recognition often have the force of a revelation. The hearing they produce is not at all something that just happens to us. It is something we do. When we hear the rain on the windowpane we don't hear it as the rain: We hear the rain. When we hear music (or anything else) express something, we hear it *as*: We hear the lighting up of a Wittgensteinian aspect; we hear it *and* we hear something else. In hearing it—and without ceasing to hear it—we hear something else.

(The figure of lighting up, of emerging from obscurity into the light, marks an important difference between Wittgenstein's *-as* structure and Heidegger's in *Being and Time*, which turns on a certain primary tautology: I see the hammer *as* a hammer.[1] Unlike Heidegger's *as*, Wittgenstein's applies to acts and utterances, not just to things in the world, and it is capable of producing the unforeseen or, in Heideggerian terms, the unforeknown. The lighting up of an aspect breaks and rebegins the hermeneutic circle.)

Hearing-as, the sounding out of an aspect, is a genre of listening. Listening in the first instance is a listening-for, a combination of waiting and sorting, of apprehending. In listening, I transform hearing, the involuntary reception of sound, into hearing-as, the simultaneous endowment and reception of what I hear under a certain aspect. After that the aspect can resound on its own; I can hear it without listening for it, or to it, even without knowing that I'm listening. Hearing records the event of sound; hearing-as opens its expressive force. In hearing music express something, hearing music *as* something, what I do is perform a hearing act—a speech act I can perform without speaking, a speech act by ear: just what my phrasing might lead you to suppose, and to ask in turn how such a counterintuitive thing could be.

This is from Wittgenstein's diary, April 28, 1930: "I often think: the highest thing I'd wish to achieve is composing a melody. Or I'm amazed that when wishing to do so, a melody has never actually occurred to me. But then

I have to say to myself that it is probably impossible that I will ever compose a melody, as I lack some or perhaps all of what it takes to do so. It floats before me as a lofty ideal, as I would then be able to more or less sum up my life; and present it, as it were, crystallized out. It would perhaps be only a small, poor crystal, but still a crystal."[2]

So the meaning of this melody that Wittgenstein can only wish to compose would be the meaning of his life. If so, then his signature idea that understanding a melody is like understanding a sentence would not apply, at least not here. One can't put the meaning of one's life into a single sentence; surely it would take at least two! This melody cannot only not be composed; it cannot be heard or even imagined. It can only be seen—as a shape? a moving form? a phantom of notation?—and seen from afar, floating before the mind's eye, not the ear, as a lofty ideal. Like the legendary music of the spheres, this melody cannot descend to audibility. Any attempt to realize it would no longer be *the* melody, for there is only one, but only another addition to the world's multitude of melodies: not a crystal, but a shard. Perhaps the hidden model here is the Wagnerian leitmotif, which has neither a fixed sound nor a fixed identity and yet always strikes the ear as a numinous whole. (But never, one must add, the ear of the one to whom it applies; Wagner's characters live their leitmotifs but do not hear them. Wagner's listeners hear what his characters can't but the listeners too have a hearing problem: they can hear phrases of music *as* the motifs but the motifs themselves remain inaudible.)

But what is it about melody that makes it possible to imagine composing one as a magic crystal? Why, after all, do we so often have the experience (and we do) that *this* melody in *this* moment really does sum up our life? Even if we have composed neither the life nor the melody?

In 1837, Robert Schumann published the set of eighteen short pieces he called *Davidsbündlertänze*: "Dances of the League of David." The league is an imaginary group of artists dedicated to opposing the spirit of Philistinism—bourgeois timidity and respectability—in the name of artistic and romantic adventure. As noted in the previous chapter, the penultimate number carries the heading "Wie aus der Ferne" (As from the Distance). But what distance is that? We might wonder: *as* what distance? As distance in time or space or depth of consciousness? As a negation of the here and now or an enrichment of it? Wittgenstein wondered too. He remarked of this music that it expresses the sense of "pastness" in the same way as the verbal phrase "long, long ago." Fair enough; the music is easy to hear in these terms. But what does such expression consist of? Who is expressing what to whom? And when? How does the expression (how does the feeling) address itself to the logic, the mad logic, of the date?

We could ask all sorts of questions about this. Was the feeling of pastness something Schumann had, or wanted to have, or read about, or thought others would have? Or is the distance really a spatial, mountain distance, and temporal only within the confines of the piece?[3] Assume for the moment that Schumann had an actual feeling, some sort of deep nostalgia, and that he "expressed" it in this music. The assumption, like Wittgenstein's remark, is fair enough, given what we know about Schumann, who would probably not have wanted to fabricate a feeling he had not experienced. Nonetheless, the assumption settles very few questions and begs many others. Did Schumann have the feeling while composing, so that the music forms a permanent record of that immediate feeling? If so, must we suppose that Schumann composed the piece at one sitting, before the feeling could expire, or, if not, that the feeling was, so to speak, portable, so that it returned with each of several compositional sessions or somehow lingered between them until the work was done? Or is the feeling one that Schumann had at another time, or had recurrently, but that in the technically demanding activity of composition he could only reproduce, or represent, or reinterpret, so that the feeling is one that the music constructs rather than records?

We're not done. What happens when someone plays the music expressively and we hear the performance? Is the performer supposed to participate in the feeling or simply to convey it, and what difference does it make that we, as audience, have no way to tell what the performer is feeling? (The performer may perform the feeling as well as the piece.) What happens when we, as would often have been the case in Schumann's day, do not passively listen to the piece but play it ourselves? What do we do when we express the feeling of nostalgia, and how does our role as performer mirror, or not, our role as perceiver? It seems hard to deny that the feeling at stake, the bittersweet nostalgia, is involved in all this, but even harder to locate it and define our relationship to it.

We might say that this difficulty is a gift. This indefiniteness is precisely what moves us about music, which gives whatever it expresses a semipermanent form but with no effect of reification. The background to this gift is the familiar opposition between the gaze, which mortifies, and the voice, which vivifies. Images freeze; music moves. When images move, they usually do so to music. The music animates feeling by filling invisibility simultaneously with both the feeling and the musical sound. The form of musical expression is a saturated invisibility.

Well and good. But if we want to do more than simply state a negative as a positive and credit music with the transformation, we need to find more specific ways to describe what happens when music expresses a feeling, or rather, precisely because music preeminently gives us reason to question the formula *this expresses that*, to describe what happens when musical expression begins to circulate with a feeling—for example—at stake. Some hints to that end turn up in Wittgenstein's text, which provides an instance that is both particular and general, that is, one that just happens, contingently, to have occurred but that at the same time can stand as a parable for musical expression as such. In other words, it is a "best example" in Ian Hacking's sense of the term: It constitutes a prototype from which other possibilities branch off radially, linked by different chains of family resemblances.[4]

Wittgenstein begins by puzzling over the sense or experience of "pastness" and observes that "feelings of pastness" do not always involve remembering something. The past may come to us as from the distance without being remembered. It may even be the distance itself, heard as the medium of a sound that comes to us. To "get clear" on the matter, Wittgenstein turns to music:

> I will examine one particular case, that of a feeling which I shall roughly describe by saying that it is the feeling of "long, long ago." These words and the tone in which they are said are a gesture of pastness. But I will specify the experience which I mean still further by saying that it is that corresponding to a certain tune (Davids Bündler Tanze—"Wie aus weiter Ferne"). I'm imagining this tune played with the right expression and thus recorded, say, for a gramophone. Then this is the most elaborate and exact expression of a feeling of pastness that I can imagine.
>
> Now should I say that hearing this tune played with this expression is in itself that particular feeling of pastness, or should I say that hearing the tune causes the feeling of pastness to arise and that this feeling accompanies the tune? I.e., can I separate what I call this experience of pastness from the experience of hearing the tune? Or, can I separate an experience of pastness expressed by a gesture from the experience of making this gesture? Can I discover something, the essential feeling of pastness, which remains after abstracting all those experiences which we might call the experiences of expressing the feeling?
>
> I am inclined to suggest to you to put the expression of our experience in place of the experience. (*BB*, 184)

There is some doubt about whether Wittgenstein's "I am inclined" is decisive or cautious,[5] but either way the suggestion he is inclined to make is embedded in his sentence. What happens when we're inclined to accept the suggestion?

Perhaps the first thing to notice here is the value of music as a test case. Although the phrase "long, long ago" is explicit in invoking pastness and the music by Schumann is not, it is the music that gives the sense of the phrase its most elaborate and exact expression. It does so because music is the medium in which the futility of separating experience from gesture is most obvious, as we can tell from the satirical undertone of Wittgenstein's insistent questions. Do we really want to say that the feeling arises as the effect of hearing a tune that it then proceeds to accompany like a faithful dog? Music lacks the Platonic potential of words; unlike "long, long ago," it cannot postulate an abstract form of pastness. But music collapses the very notion of such a form by showing how easy it is to do without anything of the kind.

For this reason it would be pointless to object that the music expresses "long, long ago" only as a gloss on the words and could not do so without them. Wittgenstein's own wording carefully avoids this implication; the expressive relationship between the music and the verbal expression is entirely reversible. One could imagine someone asking what the phrase "long, long ago" conveys and being answered by someone saying, "Something like this" (or even saying nothing at all) and sitting down at the piano to play the Schumann piece or, better yet from Wittgenstein's standpoint—more of this later—getting up to play the piece on the gramophone.

Another point to notice is that music is not only the best example of the inseparability of gesture and expression but also the binding force of that inseparability. The phrase "long, long ago" is expressive in both the words it uses and the tone in which it is spoken. The conjunction is a necessity. The expressive force of the words remains merely potential until the words are spoken (or read or imagined) in a certain tone. If gesture and expression are as inseparable in language as they are in music, that is because language as tone is already musical. Language is already saturated with expressive variations in pitch and inflection and duration and rhythm.

Writing here in English, Wittgenstein picks up on the fact that the phrases "long ago" and "long, long ago" are very different in their impact. The first is generally neutral; the second is laden with the nostalgic overtones of longing and regret. "Long, long ago" has these qualities only secondarily because it repeats a word for emphasis. The expressive value of the repetition comes in the way the vowel sounds in "long" are intoned and extended, so that the completion of the phrase comes as from a distance, across a distance, which has been absorbed into the utterance itself as verbal music. The same might be said for the German "Wie aus weiter Ferne"—as if from a great distance—the phrase by which Wittgenstein misremembers Schumann's more neutral "Wie aus der Ferne." The prolongation of the vowel sound in "weiter" collapses the arbitrary relation of signifier and signified and installs as tone the effect of breath designated by the word. The music is, so to speak, already in the breath of "weiter," which, in turn, is what the music brings to life in our hearing or our playing of it.

What, then, does it mean to say that the music, like the phrase, expresses the sense of pastness? So far we're prepared to answer that when we listen to the music in a certain way, we hear it as expressing pastness, and further that this expression is the form our listening takes as an action, in the course of being enacted. What are the implications of this answer and how does the answer bear on the wider question of descriptive realism, the relationship of expression and truth?

Both the performative quality of expression and its location in the hearing act indicate that expression, so understood, becomes meaningful more as true *to* than as true *of* something. As we have seen before, this relation of truth-to requires a strong sense in which the truth expressed is not a prior condition but the precipitate of an event that includes the expression itself. Expressions exemplify and demonstrate; they approximate; they orient and disorient; they do not state or propose. To continue with our example, it makes little sense to say that Schumann's music either signifies or symbolizes the pastness also registered in the phrase "long, long ago." There is no signification because in hearing the music I do not decode a reference to pastness as a concept or category; I partake in the sense of pastness that my listening simultaneously perceives and produces. There is no symbolization for the same reason, no bridging of a gap between the sensory and a sense, no substitution of presentation for presence. When Wittgenstein says that the music expresses the sense of "long, long ago," he is not stating a proposition but establishing a listening post, a place or device of which he can avail himself to hear the music as expressing this particular something. He is, as he tells us, making a gesture: putting the expression of our experience in place—in the place—of our experience.

The gesture is both an open invitation and a closed circuit. Closed, because the identity of expression and experience has no origin outside itself. But open, because the elements that comprise it may—no, must—derive from multiple, overdetermined sources that far exceed the gesture of the moment. The expression calls them in. Expression calls into being the condition to which it answers.

One way it does so is through the agency of precisely the kind of utterance exemplified by Wittgenstein's exclamation "long, long ago" and Schumann's inscription, "Wie aus der Ferne." These are persistent or memorable descriptions that become inseparable from the things they describe—an important but little-studied class of utterances that perhaps deserves to be classed alongside the performative and the constative on the short list of primary forms. Such acts—I call them constructive descriptions—are either accepted or declined, or, more exactly, embraced or refused; we do not deal with them neutrally.[6] Once embraced, they produce as metaphor the reality they address. Once Schumann instructs his music to be played "Wie aus der Ferne," once Wittgenstein emends that to "Wie aus weiter Ferne," the music opens the distance and enters it, in one sense or the other, even before a note is sounded.

Mediated by a constructive description, an expressive act assumes its force, its bearing on us. Embracing the description enables us to embrace the act, which, however, will then exceed the description, something we expect, desire, and even demand that it do. Met with on these terms, the expressive act does not convey a subjective state but instead embodies conditions of knowing and feeling into which we enter and in which we believe.

Into which we enter: we, too, are a part of the inseparability; we have entered into the spirit of the expression and its spirit has entered into us, an experience that leaves its mark even if subsequent critique or deconstruction divides us from it again.

In which we believe: what is expressed is neither a fantasy nor a fiction, although it is not a natural fact, either. It is a fragment of the way the world, as a world we can dwell in, comes into being.

A constructive description of music is a listening device: an example—a best example—of the means for making something audible. Two key traits of these devices, aside from their performative effectiveness, are their durability and their transferability. They may be used repeatedly and they may be replaced by surrogates. Both traits are evident in Wittgenstein's turn from the phrase "long, long ago"—not just any phrase but a haunting one, *wie aus weiter Ferne*—to its mechanical surrogate, the gramophone. In this context, performance on the gramophone has a descriptive character, since what the recording is heard to preserve is not only the music but also what, in particular, the music is heard to express. And for some reason, in this case, the fluid device of language needs to be supplemented by the rigid device of recording. We need to revisit the relevant sentences: "I'm imagining this tune played with the right expression and thus recorded, say, for a gramophone. Then this is the most elaborate and exact expression of a feeling of pastness that I can imagine."

To express the feeling of pastness, Schumann's music "Wie aus der Ferne," "Wie aus weiter Ferne," must go through three layers of articulation. The first is the source of quotation in Wittgenstein's text, namely the score, which Wittgenstein takes for granted but which we might want to describe here as a template for repetition that makes expression possible by being (to steal the phrase) elaborate and exact but never, in principle, complete. (What it leaves out is everything the performer does to interpret it.) This layer remains dormant, lifeless, until the music reaches the next layer, a performance "with the right expression." There must be a series of gestures, quite literal gestures in this case, the work of hands moving over the keyboard, weaving the sound together, that matches the template and thus frees it from its purely abstract existence on the page. Yet this performance is not as elaborate or as exact as it could be. Because it is transient, like all live music, it is doomed to dwindle from a presence to a mere impression; the music's expressiveness will wear away as its performance fades into memory.

To counter this lapse, enter the gramophone. Memory must be averted if the impression of pastness is to become present. For that to happen, the fleeting presence of the music requires a technological aid, an archive device. This is the third layer: the recording on the gramophone. Storage and retrieval, database: the gramophone does not make the passing moment of performance permanent, but it does make it repeatable. The gramophone can recapture the past at will. Its capacity to do so is perhaps responsible for the implicit assumption that the gramophone also captures the "live" sound of the piano with perfect fidelity, which it certainly could not do when Wittgenstein was writing, but which he was far from alone in hearing. And although this would be so with any recorded performance, it is doubly so in this case, where the music achieves its fullest expression of pastness precisely by being fixed in, or as, a repeatable, recapturable past.

In one sense this intervention is perplexing. Why do we need the techno-logical supplement? Music once performed can be retrieved from memory by being performed again. Why does the expression of pastness reach its most elaborate and most exact form in the medium of its mechanical reproduction? Why take the pianist out of the picture (Wittgenstein never mentions one; the music just gets played) and turn to a machine for producing disembodied sound? Why is the most expressive performance one that is repeated without error, without decay, and without location—an acousmatic phantom? Why, for that matter, on the gramophone as opposed to the radio?

Why, in short, should the music become more, not less, expressive, when it comes as from a great distance from its "live," natural sound? The implicit answer is that it becomes more expressive as we move toward pure sound and away from the visible sources of the music in notation and performance. This remains true despite the considerable bulk of the machine. When Wittgenstein was writing, the equipment was often supposed to make itself invis-ible—literally to fade into the woodwork. Gramophone companies often marketed their products as fine furniture whose high-quality sound merged with the sensuous and social value of polished cabinetry. The effect of the gramophone is to efface itself and idealize the music. The idealization allows the quality of musical expression to seem like something essential, not like the product of a performance that could always have gone badly, a perfor-mance with the wrong expression or with no expression at all. The inferiority of the radio becomes clear in this connection if, as in Wittgenstein's day, it is mainly a device for broadcasting "live" performance, with all the attendant uncertainties.

The idealizing effect of the gramophone depends on foreclosing uncer-tainty. The recorded performance is not simply over but *safely* over; it comes already certified as having the right expression, the "soulful" quality that Wittgenstein speaks of elsewhere. Expression thus subsumes and surpasses the technological medium of its realization. That it does so is precisely how we recognize it as expression. And this is as true for the machinery of the piano as it is for the medium of phonographic recording that goes piano playing one better. Expression requires a technology of archive and retrieval to keep it from fading into mere memory, if not into oblivion. But at the same time the persistence of memory outside the archive—for we *do* remember, and memory is always already faded—imparts a certain incompleteness or anxiety to the original expression. There are no such worries with the gramo-phone, and that, we might want to say, is the limitation of sound recording.

Genuinely full expression requires the risk of loss and error. Wittgenstein (of all people) surely knows that; his point is that the risk cannot be archived. Hence the cumulative form of his description: "Then this is the most elaborate and exact expression of a feeling of pastness that I can imagine." In this sense, a sense that ripples back from the archive to its sources, expression happens fully only *after* it has happened already: expression is reexpression. Listening is the device on which this retroactive formation is recorded and played back.

But to become really "elaborate and exact," the expression requires another apparatus, though one not often thought of as such. The music played and recorded with the right expression conveys the same sense of pastness as the phrase "long, long ago." Or rather, since we can't plausibly speak of "the" sense of pastness, the music conveys a certain sense of pastness in something like the manner of the phrase, or, to be even more elaborate and exact ourselves, it intercepts and appropriates one or more of the ways of hearing that phrase as permeated by what it describes. However we describe the process, the expression cannot complete itself without a word.

That is, a word for Wittgenstein, who in this case comes close to the position of Heidegger: "Without the word, no thing is."[7] We need both to recognize, that is, to reaffirm this power of creation in the word and to locate it precisely in relation to the register of expression. The process will, as a long tradition would predict, also locate the boundary of the inexpressible—which, like the limits of old flat maps showing the edges of the world, is not really a locality at all.

In one sense the call for a word frames the situation too narrowly. The emphasis in Wittgenstein's own writing on tone, gesture, attitude (both position and disposition), and face—the cardinal elements of the register of expression—repeatedly shows us as much. These are not devices added to language but part of the device of language, parts of the devising that *is* language. Even if no one speaks, the word is never absent. There is no register of expression without it; without the word no thing is *shown*.

The word is the means by which a complex transition is enacted. It is the anchor point of a continuous circulation among the expressive modes. Expressive acts (the turns, the tropes, of tone, gesture, attitude, and face) occur in the place where language arrives: where it has arrived before, may yet arrive, will arrive, is about to arrive, will have arrived. The site of expressive performance is always also the site of performative utterance. And that site is not *one* place; it is everyplace. It is polytopia. For if the expression of a certain sense just *is* that sense (the music expresses pastness in being heard as expressing pastness), then we grasp that expression when we repeat it otherwise, when we reexpress it in another form or mode, as trope or translation, condensation or extension, reiteration or application. The repetition may be subtle or even unnoticed, an expressive act we perform almost without knowing it. The only requirement is that the repetition must belong to the extended circuit of semantic enactments, productions of meaning as "force" in Austin's sense—something we can still agree to call "illocutionary" force even if gesture, tone, or attitude are its relevant media—within which we continually engage with each other.

The reexpressive act (with music, a hearing act) is a supplement that places the perceptual event under a description. This placement is where the word becomes pivotal. Although the description does not have to be verbalized or even verbal, the model for it is verbal and it can always be indicated verbally. (Schumann seized on the possibility: "Wie aus der Ferne." The words themselves form a kind of numinous particle precipitated by the music; they are as much a hushed exclamation as an instruction.) When that happens, the sense or experience involved becomes available to interpretation. It begins to become intelligible, to engage in a mutual address with the circuit of utterances that constitute the scene of intelligibility as much (or more) by their tendency and tonality as by their substance. ("Aus weiter Ferne," Wittgenstein added, a slip of the pen or act of creative forgetting that is also an interpretation, a correction, and an appropriation. The words are as much a sigh as a (mis)quotation. The distance has grown; the music, almost too faint to discern, comes from the world of long, long ago. *Schöne Welt, wo bist du?* Only the gramophone keeps this music audible, like a telephone line to the past.) The meaning thus produced shows itself most arrestingly via a change of aspect or release of numinous particles. Or it shows itself by a kind of implicit ellipsis, a tacit request for another word, a paraphrase, a transposition, a reuse.

What it does *not* do is become fixed in or by a proposition. Meaning is not a formula, not a signified, but the orienting force of an activity of utterance. The expressive exchange does not have a transcendental term, the master term to its doglike fidelity, but it does have an uninterpreted and irreducible remainder. The remainder expresses itself as a felt potentiality, the already present futurity of the expression's later occasions and transcriptions.

In its general form, expressive exchange haloes experience with a faint but continuous resonance. It emits the background hum of a world animated by concern, the half-discernible undertone of being. Imagine its absence—say a world of toneless speech and gestureless bodies—and expressive exchange quickly stands revealed as the condition of possibility for endowing things with meaning. Particular exchanges come about through semantic performatives that light up whatever aspect marks the *as* that we hear in music or see in a face. If I follow Wittgenstein and hear "pastness" in "Wie aus der Ferne," I hear the music *as* the expression of the peculiar sense of pastness also intimated by the phrase "long, long ago." That aspect then forms a nodal point from which meaning spreads throughout a network of other locales with proliferating aspects. There is no simple way to say this, though the effect in experience is often utterly direct. The *–as* structure of perception is the nonverbal correlate of the verbal *as* or *as if* that subtends all verbalization of expressed sense from exclamation through constructive description to interpretive discourse with its paraphrases and parables. Language, especially when it rises to constructive description, is the destination but not the goal of the expressive process.

Once something, say a piece of music, is explicitly described, even if only by a phrase like "the sense of pastness," the expression becomes "elaborate and exact"—even when the initiating words are not yet either one. Bodily movement and snatches of musical memory may also initiate or prolong this effect, but only the performative circuit, the nexus of expressive performance and performative language (rainbow, arc, bridge, curvature, sweep, rhythm), can complete it. Any movement among these alternatives contributes to the performance of a hearing act. Music we might listen to or play in live performance needs the magic of performative endowment to limit the disappearance that consumes all music heard, no matter as what, in real time. The music's expressive character resides neither in the acoustic details nor in the performative act that bears witness to them but in the identity that overtakes both sound and act, in the last instance sound and word, the experience of each in the place of the other. The archival value of the recording in Wittgenstein's example is its preservation of that identity.

These technological reflections have another odd implication. Wittgenstein's reliance on the gramophone for exactness and elaboration substitutes writing with sound for writing with words. If the gramophone speaks so clearly of pastness, the depths of long, long ago, a philosopher might seem to be relieved of that burden. Whatever needs to be said, and something must, since meaning is in question, the gramophone can say it. From a historical point of view, we might take this as an insight into the nature of the machine, a response to the character of sound recording when it still seemed semi-miraculous. But can we rest content with that? We need to shift the angle of the example from expression to truth.

The expression preserved via the sound-writing of the gramophone belongs neither to the music nor to its performance but to the preservation of the one by the other. Insofar as the live music was true to what it expressed, the recording preserves that fidelity by preserving the music's sound. What the recording records is not the sound but the truth of the expression. Wittgenstein says so in so many words. What the gramophone plays is a hearing act. In some sense the sound, with its acoustic virtues and defects, just gets in the way. But at every stage of the process the effect of the expression is not one of truth to a pure origin, not the intact transmission of a preexisting sense of pastness. On the contrary, the effect is the origination of a certain truth, a sense of pastness that could not otherwise be grasped, not even in the utterance of its verbal twin, "long, long ago." Wittgenstein's gramophone is a truth machine. That's why its expression is elaborate and exact. But of what and with respect to what? What truth does the gramophone's expression intimate?

The truth of "pastness" is still Wittgenstein's answer. This is not a logical tautology to be avoided but a lived tautology to be embraced. Its strangeness is part of the blessing of the ordinary, or becomes so once we content ourselves with recognizing that the expression of the sense of pastness *is* that sense. But this is less the "true" answer than the promise or potential of one. We may all agree to hear a temporal distance in Schumann's piece but we can hardly rest content with that without falling back into an ideology of the ineffable. "Pastness" is a poor paraphrase even of "long, long ago"; it operates in Wittgenstein's text like a surrogate for a meaning understood but not articulated. The turn to Schumann doubles the surrogate effect, as if pastness were being entrusted to a medium in which its ineffableness would not be questioned. The medium is overdetermined—not just music, but piano music, the vehicle of shared self-expression, and *Schumann's* piano music, the music of esoteric private inwardness. The gramophone fixes this effect by fixing the right expressive performance of the music. The meaning of "long, long ago," which is also the music's meaning, becomes identical with its place in a sound archive, the possibility of its retrieval from a database. Retrieval takes the place of interpretation.

But should we let it? *Can* we let it, even in the unlikely case that we can be satisfied with only the one properly expressive performance? (If there is one, there must be others; if there were not, there could not be the one.) The music is supposed to express the feeling of pastness exactly and to elaborate on it. If the music really does that, we should be able to say how. And we should be able to say what. Our perception of the music *as* something is a perception of it as meaningful, and one meaning always cntails a plurality of others; hearing-as is both prolific and intelligible. In this case, the Heideggerian formulation also applies: The music we hear as this or that is interpreted in being heard and thus subject to continued interpretation along the course of the hermeneutic circle. If Schumann's "Wie aus der Ferne" expresses pastness, it does so only by disturbing our understanding of pastness. It acts like a stone dropped in a pond, rippling the water in every direction to the edges of vision. (A musical example, really: The stone strikes with a tone; the water vibrates like a tympanum.) We may never make our understanding of this process wholly or even partly explicit; we may grasp it only indirectly or figuratively or in qualitative flashes, but it should be available in principle. Available doubly: to deliberate reflection as something to be interpreted, and to direct experience as something to partake of or perform.

How does Schumann's musical version of "long, long ago" do in this regard?

To answer that, we must first ask another question, obvious perhaps to us but virtually inaudible to Wittgenstein: Why Schumann? Why, that is, a work of classical music, apart from the fact that for Wittgenstein "music" and the classical tradition were virtually synonymous? Popular music, particularly popular song, has an uncanny ability to suggest pastness simply by surviving its own moment of origin; we can recapture something of the texture of an earlier time, an echo of its structure of feeling, by listening to its songs, especially perhaps in the recorded voices of the time and the "voice" of its recording technology. But to that kind of pastness Wittgenstein seems deaf or indifferent.

The traditional protocol for listening to classical music called for hearing it as outside any history but musical history. Any "pastness" the music might express would have no location, no calendar; it would not be the pastness of this time or that but only of long, long ago. For Wittgenstein, the only "pastness" to be evoked by a classical work would be that of an ideal former age, an idyllic era that cannot be remembered because it was never experienced, a pastness inaccessible except through such music as might address the listener "wie aus der Ferne." In "Wie aus der Ferne," Wittgenstein heard the sense of the past as epochal and uniform rather than as historical and discontinuous.

But although the music could readily provide the legendary sense of "long, long ago" for which he was listening—we will see why—there remains the question of why *that* sense, rather than a sense of the historical past, was what he was listening for. The answer has to do with the form of listening that classical music both asks for and makes available.

In *Why Classical Music Still Matters*, I suggested that this form or order of listening is that of the modern subject whose identity is coterminous with its self-estrangement. Confronted with the appeal or injunction to listen absorbedly—with speech acts like "Listen to me!" "Listen closely," "I want you to listen to me," "Are you listening?"—the subject must do more than simply recognize, understand, and even heed. This subject must both open itself and concentrate itself. It must find the wherewithal to be especially receptive to what must be heard, no matter how discomfiting or decentering that may prove, and at the same time it must hold fast to its own agency and its ability to reply. I called this sort of hearing *hearkening*. It might also be identified as the mode of hearing we seek when we listen for the truth. Starting no later than the mid-eighteenth century, what we now call classical music was designed to model and provoke such hearkening, and that remains its principal cultural value, even if other musical genres later ventured into the same territory by different means. For Wittgenstein, Schumann's "Wie aus der Ferne" expressed the sense of the past by allowing or inducing him to hearken to the sense of pastness. Just what that meant we can surmise by hearkening ourselves with Wittgenstein's hearing in mind. We will not be able to recover exactly what he heard for ourselves; the listening involved is itself too "dated" for that. But we can still reenter and extend the network of hearing-as in which different senses of the past accomplish themselves through this music.

How, then, *does* Schumann's musical version of "long, long ago" do in this regard?

The theme Wittgenstein refers to arises indistinctly over a deep pedal tone and an inner-voice pedal softly pulsating off the beat. "Wie aus der Ferne" thus begins—but it doesn't begin, it emerges out of the indeterminate end of the previous piece, which doesn't really end. So the piece "begins": it emerges by breaking into a cloud of numinous particles. No sooner has a wisp of melody sounded in the treble than it assumes a murmuring indistinct form by dipping below the pulsation and sounding again in the bass (see Example 5.1). The melody, in other words, sinks into the distance from which it also returns. As it does so, its tone and texture assume an indefiniteness

EXAMPLE 5.1 Schumann, "Wie aus der Ferne," no. 17 of *Davidsbündlertänze*, mm. 1–37

EXAMPLE 5.1 (*Continued*)

that adds, metaphorically, a sense of distance and pastness to its sound. So the music, for many measures, sounds like something heard long, long ago. And because it does, hearing this music assumes the uncanny form of rehearing it even if one has never heard it before. Eventually this distant music fades away into another distance—the distance from, or nearly from, the origin. It fades into a repetition of the second piece of the cycle. This new act of retrieval from a distance, of something nameable, bounded, and, so to speak, calendrical, may thus appear to rest on the foundation of the earlier, more inward retrieval as on something spellbinding: nameless, boundless, and primordial.

Moreover—and this is the point at which expression seeks to become a constructive description, to embody a certain truth—because the drift of the passage is from hearing to rehearing, from distinction to indistinction, from now to then, the sense of the past expressed here is one that operates as a secret, beckoning, perhaps disorienting subtext to the sense of presence. This, the music suggests, is how the past persists, offering itself even as it withdraws: *wie aus der Ferne*. In Heideggerian terms we might say that the music embodies the sending, the gift, the *es gibt* of being, which, he tells us, always holds something back in the giving.

Even a music that expressed a sense of the historical past would operate this way; this modality of pastness is the concrete form of a theory of historical being. And so, to catch at the quality of the still-present past at its secretive, uncanny work, we might find a word like *pastness* or the common phrase *long ago* inadequate. We might need to proffer the more chantlike, reiterative "long, long ago." The words, in such a case, do not signify or specify, but precisely express—without expressing precisely—what the experience of the still-present past has brought as from the distance.

Schumann was tempted to make a similar proffer, though he famously withdrew it from the second edition of the score. "Wie aus der Ferne" remains present after it "ends," which it does not really do; it melts away on the dominant, withdraws at a moment of incompletion, and hovers latently behind what follows, the reprise of the second piece. The reprise "resolves" the dominant with an interruption that shifts to a different mode of pastness. The past retrieved here is built on the pastness of "Wie aus der Ferne," but is also remote from it; it is a revisited past, no longer uncanny and indefinite— the temporal equivalent of a return to an old haunt. And although the reprise now segues into a coda that brings both the piece (but then again, which piece?) and the cycle to what seems like a very definite end, the still-present past has not stopped resounding. It persists into another number, the last at last, linked to "Wie aus der Ferne" doubly: first by recalling and reinterpreting a passage of augmented-sixth harmony that had mysteriously emerged amid the first distance (see Example 5.1), and then by gradually retrieving the numinous particle that is the "theme"—the melodic substance—of that distance.

The theme—but keep in mind: it is no longer a theme, just something that was one once, or rather, in this case, never quite was one, because it emerged as a numinous particle—carries the entire cycle away into the deepest bass... and silence (see Example 5.2). Or rather it waltzes away, since this end after the end is, as noted in Chapter 3, the ghost of a waltz, a dreamy recollection of a giddy romantic whirl we have never heard as such, slowed down, hypnotic, all post-. Which prompted Schumann to write, before he erased the words (and yet we still know them): "Quite superfluously Eusebius added the following; but thereby much bliss spoke out of his eyes." Spoke, that is, with a sparkle in the eyes, a musical gaze that did, and does, add itself as a blissful surplus to the sounds that have come calling as from the pastness of the past. We will see later how this musical speech act finds elaborate and exact expression in a scattering of numinous particles.[8]

And what if, with later ears, we should listen to this music's theory of the past recaptured to hear it as a Romantic dream, a fantasy of wholeness at odds with an emerging modern perception of both thought and feeling

EXAMPLE 5.2 Schumann, no. 18 of *Davidsbündlertänze* (complete)

EXAMPLE 5.2 (*Continued*)

as fragmentary, nervously irritable, and socially uncertain? These are traits expressed throughout *Davidsbündlertänze*. They are especially prominent in the number that dissolves into "Wie aus der Ferne," and in the agitated passage between the reprise of the second number and the start of the last. If we hear the music as expressing its nostalgia reactively as much, or more, as it does evocatively, we will also hear Wittgenstein's hearing as susceptible to the same defensive dream, no doubt from the position of a later and more troubled modernity. But to do that will not have obliterated Wittgenstein's hearing-as but instead will have recomposed and repositioned it. We will have changed the aspect with which pastness and distance have faced us.

But why should we trust such expression? Are we not here finding a meaning where we would be better off without one? A long tradition, fading but still in force, would say so. But here I suggest that we *not* listen, or at least not heed.

Hearkening at its most intense may rise to a sense of partaking in all-absorbing multidimensional presence without definite boundaries—the condition that Jean-Luc Nancy calls being singular plural.[9] But this presence is never unmediated, and its mediated character is never an obstruction to the arrival of presence, but, on the contrary, is precisely its means of conveyance. Listening at this level always requires some version of Wittgenstein's gramophone: the artifice, the prosthesis, of situation, word, circumstance, date, or event. To reverse Wittgenstein's dictum, listening to a melody is more like understanding a sentence than one might suspect.

Recognizing as much calls for a fundamental revision in the traditional *metaphysics* of music, a term that Nancy retrieves from Schopenhauer and a concept for which he advocates in the process of trying to reject it. At this point Nancy and Wittgenstein combine, as from a great distance (wie aus weiter Ferne), in a conceptual counterpoint. Drawn together by their deep investments in the matter of listening yet divided by the resonances they find there, the two stand at opposite ends of the spectrum of possibilities for thinking about what we do in hearing music express something. At one pole is something familiar and deeply wrong; at the opposite pole is something barely thought of but very right. In case anyone is still wondering, the thinker who has it wrong is Nancy. That leaves Wittgenstein happily in the right—but not for reasons that either thinker would imagine.

For Nancy, listening in the sense of the close, absorbed listening we have been considering involves us in "an intimacy more intimate than any evocation or any invocation"; the ineffability of music—and note that he simply assumes this ineffability without question or reflection—"does not constitute an oversignification but, on the contrary, a beyond-significance [outre-signifiance] that it is not possible to enter and analyze under any kind of code"—and note the unreflective subsumption of participation and analysis under the rubric of code, and the concurrent bypassing of any hermeneutic engagement. (Nancy's "beyond-significance" is too close to Lacan's "the beyond-signified" [le hors-signifie] as a name for the Thing not to be playing on it.[10] But Nancy's musical Thing is strangely accessible—which would not have surprised Schopenhauer.) There is, of course, one exception to this nonsignifying delirium, namely "musical codes, which, precisely, are not semantic, not linguistic, and that are also not determinable as a 'language of affects' in the proper sense of such an expression."[11]

Typically for those who take this position, Nancy assumes that any involvement of the semantic or linguistic or affective immediately negates the musicality of music, as if these modes of representation could not be plurally singular together with music as heard presence, and as if music as heard presence were the only way of experiencing music. Thus for Nancy, "What truly betrays music and diverts or perverts the movement of its modern history is the extent to which it is indexed to a mode of signification and not to a mode of sensibility."[12] His paradigmatic example of this betrayal is one that flatly identifies musical signification with both the soullessness of the machine and the worst evils of the twentieth century: "one could say that [Beethoven's] Ninth Symphony derives its meaning . . . from the fact of being played in a Panzer factory, in the presence of those valiant workers who are forming . . . modern images of Teutonic knighthood."[13] "Meaning" in this quotation must be pronounced with a sneer; for Nancy, meaning is simply synonymous with the faithful-dog idea of expression. Wittgenstein's gramophone, it would seem, is just a toy panzer, and his sense of the distant past in Schumann's "Wie aus dem Ferne" conceals a regressive nostalgia for epic brutality. Never mind that as a matter of history, the nonsemantic, nonlinguistic dimension of music was precisely what apologists for Teutonic supremacy claimed as uniquely their own.

For Nancy, true listening occurs only when "it is not a hearer who listens . . . Listening is musical when it is music that listens to itself. It returns to itself, it reminds itself of itself, and it feels itself as resonance itself: a relationship to self deprived, stripped, of all egoism and all ipseity."[14] In other words, music is the negation of human agency, identity, and responsibility. You—but we should not speak of "you" and "I"—you, yes, you: You listen to music best when you deny your personhood and your historical being and literally become an instrument through which music reflects on its own continuous unfolding. In music, self is reduced to the reflexivity embodied in the phrase form "it . . . itself." Unlike Wittgenstein, for whom music, like language, like gesture, like action, is embedded in a dizzying plurality of living practices, Nancy represents music as a kind of living death, although he would surely deny the attribution and dismiss it as a misunderstanding. Unlike Wittgenstein, Nancy fails to understand that in listening there is always a gramophone—always, that is, a prosthetic form, something other than music through which music comes to life.

Even Nancy's ideal scene of listening contains such a prosthesis. If music properly heard is what listens to itself *through me*, then I am the connector, the apparatus, the gramophone that makes this self-listening come about. I am the relay that returns or refers the music to itself. To do so, I must empty out my own self—a dubious possibility and an even more dubious demand—so that my own necessary presence may become imperceptible, forgettable. More precisely, my bodily sentience becomes the apparatus for recording and playing back the music to itself while my being in every other register, not only as some *one* who feels (Nancy's criterion of self) but also as one who knows and speaks and expresses, is effaced in an act of what might best be described as aesthetic asceticism.

Music thus becomes an instrument in the campaign waged by Nancy and others in his intellectual tradition against Being, appropriation, and "ipseity," an issue that can be touched on only indirectly here. But surely Nancy's ideal scene of listening is a travesty of the normal circumstance in which we act as if music were connecting one person to another and perhaps to many others. Music as an aesthetic mode draws us, in our overlapping roles of composers, performers, and listeners, into a rich public/private intimacy, what Nancy himself might call a partaking or sharing of the musical event. But other people, at least "in person," are strangely lacking in Nancy's text. The irreducibly social character of expression, the speech act, the language game, omnipresent in Wittgenstein despite the countervailing impression of a solitary mind continually addressing itself, is dissolved there in favor of a ritualistic syncope embodied by the idealization of timbre. Ruled out is musical expression, the very medium of connection. And with that, the question we started with (*What do we do in hearing music express something?*) gets a simple answer: We misunderstand what we hear.

We might reply by saying that, on the contrary, we understand precisely what we hear. We understand the music. That is the form that understanding music takes. But what do we understand by saying *that*?

Wittgenstein returned several times to his statement that understanding a sentence is like understanding a melody. It seems to have been important to him, not least because he felt he needed to clarify what the statement expressed. He apparently needed to understand *this* sentence, which appealed to him like a melody and, like a melody, carried its meaningfulness in advance of its meaning.

Here is an extended passage, again written in English, which works around to such a clarification from an unlikely starting point, the mystique of music's ineffability. This is an idea that Wittgenstein's own investigations should have led him to reject. And so he did—though without quite admitting it:

> If repeating a tune to ourselves and letting it make its full impression on us, we say, "This tune *says* something," . . . it is as though I had to find *what* it says. And yet I know it doesn't say anything such that I might express in words or pictures what it says. [But I—LK—want to say: melody speaks and yet withholds speech in this way only if we let it make its full impact on us. We have to *admit* it into the terrain of its own enigmatic character, which is its resonance in our hearing.] And if, recognizing this, I resign myself to saying, "It just expresses a musical thought," this would mean no more than saying, "It expresses itself."—"But surely when you play it you don't play it just *anyhow*, you play it in a particular way, making a crescendo here, a diminuendo there, a caesura in this place, etc." Precisely, and that's all I can say about it, or may be all. . . . For in certain cases I can justify, explain the particular expression with which I play by a comparison, as when I say . . . "This is, as it were, the answer to what came before," etc. . . .
>
> This doesn't mean that suddenly understanding a musical theme may not consist in finding a form of verbal expression which I conceive as the verbal counterpart of the theme. And in the same way I may say, "Now I understand the expression of this face," and what happened when the understanding came was that I found the word which seemed to sum it up.
>
> Consider also the expression: "Tell yourself it's a *waltz*, and you will play it correctly."
>
> What we call "understanding a sentence" has, in many cases, a much greater similarity to understanding a musical theme than we might be inclined to think. [LK: Inclined, because the separation of music from words and pictures—the latter compounded into a general form, the imagetext—is the very condition of intelligibility as it is traditionally understood.] But I don't mean that understanding a musical theme is more like the picture one tends to make oneself of understanding a sentence, but rather that this picture is wrong, and that understanding a sentence is much more like what really happens when we understand a tune. . . . For understanding a sentence, we say, points to a reality outside the sentence. Whereas we might say "Understanding a sentence means getting hold of its content; and the content of the sentence is *in* the sentence" (*BB*, 166–67).

I want to reweave three threads drawn from this passage:

1. That what a melody expresses can't be translated into words is a cliché and almost a definition. But this opacity takes on a new aspect if we split it into two observations that we then recombine: first, that the melody can't (of course) be translated but then that in some sense it *should* be. The effect of the melody is to evade a translation that it not only invites but also seems to

demand. We hear it almost as if we once knew the translation but have some-how forgotten it. We owe it (as debt or duty) a translation we can never provide.

2. In response we drift, or drive, as the passage does, toward verbal coun-terparts: an analogy, a summarizing word, or a gestural surrogate. And it is not so much the verbal expression as the act of finding it that produces, that performs, the understanding. There is no question here of translation at all, but only one of "getting hold" of a content *in* the melody by living, as we do, *with* the melody—playing it in a certain way, pairing it with a word or phrase. It is not that the melody expresses what we understand by it, but that we under-stand what we hear it express. This understanding takes the form of a percep-tual transformation, not in what we perceive but in how. When Wittgenstein writes, "Tell yourself it's a *waltz*, and you will play it correctly," the implied intonation (in the italics, in the imperative voice) expresses the fact that the melody seemed otherwise at first. The understanding and the word are bound together in a mutual arrival that they simultaneously witness and produce. This arrival takes the specific form of a musical performance, or more exactly of its possibility—that we either do, or become able to, play (or hum, or whistle, or hear) the melody in a new way that strikes us as right. The performative utter-ance, the expressive action, shows the understanding that is *in* it.

3. But this does not mean that understanding exhausts itself in the act of performance or in a few impromptu words. Wittgenstein's preoccupation with words and sentences gets in his way here and brings the understanding he describes to a premature closure. His own example betrays him: "Tell yourself it's a *waltz*," a genre (sometimes a dance, sometimes an abstract form) almost too richly packed with cultural, social, national, sexual, and romantic connotations, a virtual paradigm of the power of an expressive mark to draw understanding into an ever-expanding network of traces and associations—to open hermeneutic windows at every turn. The result of local expressive acts, the kind that Wittgenstein takes as his models, is not to confine but to free us, not to make us terse but to make us voluble.

This volubility brings us around one last time to our leitmotif of a ques-tion: What do we do in hearing music express something?

The answer turns out to be that—we answer. We express something back. Like Wittgenstein's gramophone, we both archive the expressive action and repeat it with a certain difference. The difference is a mode of interpretation that we can, if we choose, reflect on and extend, or else, if we choose, simply enjoy. Either way, what we enjoy is a meaning—not a meaning tied to the music as by a leash or worse, but a meaning that is, or rather becomes, the music's meaning, a meaning we enjoy in hearing the music. More often than not, perhaps, we make our expressive answer in a highly condensed, relatively inarticulate form, perhaps one that we scarcely notice. "Long, long ago" is an example just long enough—the repetition in the phrase is necessary—but having once been said it can be condensed further into a nonverbal mnemonic, say a certain tilt of the head or a literal backward glance. At other times, we may poise ourselves to answer without actually doing so, and thus experience our apprehension, our grasp, of the musical expression as a form of readiness, even if it is only a readiness to hum or sing or whistle a melody with something like the appropriate expression. For Wittgenstein, the preferred medium was whistling; he could whistle whole movements of Beethoven symphonies. Whatever the medium, though, the circuit of expression has to be closed or there is no expression at all. Nancy's ideal scene of listening is entirely inexpressive—a condition he might not object to—because expression expresses nothing until an answer is forthcoming.

The expressive answer is not a signifier of meaning. It just *is* a meaning in condensed form, or, alternatively conceived, it is a demonstration of meaning—a showing or offering—that touches on what it shows. Essential to this conception is the realization that the answer is neither the limit of meaning nor a restricted, minimally articulate sort of meaning that is disconnected in principle from hermeneutic expansion. On the contrary, meaning in the hermeneutic sense may always be extrapolated from an expressive answer, though we may often be content to rest with the mere possibility. In reverse, as incorporation, the same process allows hermeneutic meaning to show itself, to express itself, in the concentrated form of the answer. Any point in this network leads to every other.

Is music ineffable? Of course. What isn't? Who ever supposed that language could exhaust or replace the experiences or sensations, even the texts, that it addresses? In this sense music is beyond significance in the same way that language is. Meaning is not a fixed or assignable statement; far less is it a signified. Meaning is the vanishing point of a discourse, the orienting force of a semantic performance that has always already begun and has no definite ending.

But is music *the* beyond-significance? The beyond, that is, of meaning in any sense but perceptual cohesion, and sometimes beyond even that? Sometimes. We do have certain forms of life, certain language games that allow us to hear music that way. But what we hear in that case is not music as such, but music in one of its myriad guises. We *place* music beyond significance, most likely so that we can place ourselves there and find relief from the worldly weight of meaning, which is sometimes too heavy. It would be glib to say that this act of dividing music from meaning is itself a meaning we impart to music. But it is not glib to recognize that this act of placement or dis-placement is not a simple product of musical perception but rather an expressive reply that enables the music to assume a concrete expressive value in or as the beyond-significance. In that respect, denuding music of meaning is no different from any other act of expressive answering. But perhaps it is an answer we should give with less readiness and more irony.

Does music even *want* to be the beyond-significance? Can we not hear certain pieces, at certain moments, as expressing a contrary desire, and even a critique of the desire for any such supposed beyond? The last number of *Davidsbündlertänze* suggests that we can. We can hear as much if we reply to it in more detail than we have before.

The piece evolves by reiterating the light tracery of its waltz rhythm via little touches or splashes of sound in different registers. The player's arms and hands move in a pattern that seems continuously to weave the music together from these bits of sonorous material (see Example 5.2). As part of the process, certain dissonances accumulate, especially seconds—some tied, some sounded. Most of them resolve well enough, but there are so many of them, and they sound so transparently, that resolution becomes not the means to integrate them but rather a way simply to hear them better. What becomes most audible is the way the music defers resolution by letting the traces of its dissonances linger through exposed rests from one measure to another, a process that eventually expands to cover a whole passage; or, elsewhere, the way the dissonant pulses cluster so thickly that "resolving" them is beside the point and the music momentarily stops bothering with it (mm. 11–20). More and more the dissonant squibs become irreducible parts of the dispersed whole.

The recurrence of these dissonances is anything but disturbing. Their presence amounts to an offer, a gift, of the present itself, a present no longer haunted by the lure of distance. The dissonances, especially the seconds, are not there to disappear but, precisely, to appear as numinous particles. The music luxuriates in them. It presents them in the lulling nonurgency of its unhurried tempo and the hypnotic reweaving motion of the player's hands. (*Nicht schnell*, says Schumann in the second edition: not fast, linger here. The tempo is the trace of Eusebius's bliss; the first edition had no tempo marking.[15]) These caressing "dissonances" (does the term still apply?) eventually become the medium for the reexpression of the "distant melody," which returns—not too soon; like the tempo, the event is *nicht schnell*—for a series of fragmentary encores after the music has filled with its absence. The melody almost catches itself by surprise. It returns changed, a wisp of itself, and at first it seems only a fleeting remnant (mm. 31–33). But then it returns to linger, to let itself waltz a little, and as it does it mingles increasingly with the warm sound of the seconds in the middle register (mm. 39–50). This mingling is both an act of crystallization and an act of self-surrender. For the melody also returns under a description of farewell, the *Abschied* of its ebbing away, only a moment later, into the depths of the bass.

This music is "superfluous" not because it is unnecessary but because it literally overflows the boundaries of near and far, past and present. Its lack of formal necessity is precisely what makes it expressively necessary. It is explicitly a musical speech act that revokes the beyond, that returns the distance into the distance, that calls on the voice of the past only to speak the "bliss" of its present utterance. Or to let bliss speak, as Schumann's metaphor would have it: as if to say "long, long ago" with a waltzlike lilt. The bliss is situated at the exact site where the magical, creative power of the word arises, even (always) before the word does. That site becomes audible when you hear, and palpable when you play, those glimmering seconds.

"Tell yourself it's a *waltz*. . . ." The moment we recognize that listening is not a natural process but something devised, that hearing-as always requires a hearing aid, we are cast willy-nilly into the world of constructive descriptions and confronted with the principle, the demand, the opportunity, of expressive reciprocity: to grasp an expression is to give one back. As music tells us paradigmatically, we fully understand an expressive act only when we return it. If we do nothing, we are not beyond meaning but before it. When we do something, even if it is no more than to quicken our step or mutter "long, long ago," what we do connects us to a community of meanings to which there is no beyond.

So: To receive an expression is to return it. But to be able to return it, one must be a participant in its way of working, to feel what it gives to know and know what it gives to feel. And to do that, one must ally oneself with neither the feeling nor the knowledge but with the activity of moving between the one and the other. Jacques Rancière suggests that to participate in that activity is to tell a story about it: "The economy of knowledge has to be predicated on a story. This does not mean an illusion or a lie. It means it is predicated on an operation that weaves the fabric within which the articulation of the knowledges can be believed, within which it can operate."[16] The result is neither truth nor fiction but a livable knowledge precipitated from the predication of each on the other.

To this epistemic neither/nor I would add an aesthetic one, a variant of the neither/nor framework I adapted from Ranciére in Chapter 3. One pole of this reexpressed neither/nor is occupied by narrative itself, the other by music. All art vacillates between the tendencies represented by these terms—including the arts of narrative and music. To return an expression sent along the arc of either tendency is to navigate the neither/nor between the two, to produce a livable knowledge by predicating each on the other.

Narrative is the representation of event as trajectory and sequence, usually rendered intelligible in retrospect. It determines itself with regard (in every sense of the term) to external actions, actions outside the narrative, which it treats as if real whether to record that reality (history) or merely to simulate it (fiction). Narrative in this sense is an ideal type, meaning that it forms a model for narrative practice in general even though that practice often departs from or complicates the model, perhaps as often or more often, even much more often, than not. This departure is the becoming-music of narrative, a system of internal echoes and allusions, doublings and tropings, references and positionings, intimating a whole that is detached from, independent of, the events narrated.

Conversely, music is an elaboration of such a purely internal determination whether or not it is also a representation or expression on the one hand or the agency of a institutional process (social, religious, military, courtly, commercial) on the other. Music in this sense is also an ideal type, and just as disposed as narrative is to departures and complications that form the becoming-narrative of music.

The movement between these alternatives is not oppositional in principle, although it can become so in practice. The becoming-musical, including the becoming-musical of music, is what endows the artwork with aesthetic value, allows the work to give pleasure merely in being perceived. To render aesthetic is to render musical. The becoming-narrative, including the becoming-narrative of narrative, is what endows the artwork with a concrete content. To render narrative is to render topical. Traditional debates about the aesthetic treat these tendencies as antagonistic and assign judgments of truth or morality to the side of narrative and judgments of skill and pleasure to the side of music. The result is a debate that was already sterile when Plato started it in Book X of the *Republic* and proposed to exile overly musical poets from the ideal city-state.

There is never a legitimate choice between the narrative and the musical, only the choice of how to linger in the interval between them. It is precisely this lingering, and not the resolution to one mode or another, that is the distinctive property of the artwork as such. The distinctive form of the aesthetic neither/nor is the wandering movement of reexpression in which the musical assumes cognitive value and the narrative seeks the support of musical pleasure. This reciprocity, by no means always successful or innocent, and only easy when it is mendacious, is for better and worse the source of the social and conceptual import of the aesthetic.

Musicality thus lays claim to an importance rarely accorded it. And since this musicality is at its most acute in actual music, in sounding music and its archive of notation and recording, the work of understanding music takes on a new urgency and a new mandate. We can no longer regard music as a background or accompaniment to the work of cognition, no longer treat it as something we love and admire but do not, in the end, take fully seriously because we cannot, in the end, bring ourselves to treat even the most admired music as more than a sublime pastime. It is past time for this to stop. We can no longer philosophize without music, and must learn to philosophize with music.

Among philosophers, it is not Wittgenstein but Theodor Adorno who knew this best and banked on it most. But Wittgenstein is still perhaps the better model, because he allowed music more independent agency, and with it more quirkiness and more strangeness, than did Adorno, for whom music, however much could be learned from it, always remained a symptom of a prior (and a dire) condition. Adorno heard all music as an implicit dirge for the death of subjectivity, a powerful conception but a narrow one. He is forever haunted by the specter of separability that Wittgenstein banishes, not to wave the spectral world away, but to restore it in the fullness of its strangeness. What Wittgenstein knew, and could not quite bring himself to say but constantly showed, is that the strangeness of living entangled in the forms of expressive life is far more luxuriant and more creative than the supposed realm of abstract mind could ever be. Music expresses this knowledge all the time, but never the same way twice.

The question of the aesthetic is not one but two, of which the first is hard and the second still harder, so much so that it has rarely been asked, much less answered. The first question: What kind of knowledge do we achieve when we embrace that which gives pleasure in perception alone as an expressive act?

(The question assumes, rudely enough, that the traditional answer, "none," is not worth a second thought.) The second: What does it mean to live in a world where pleasure can be had in perception alone? What does that tell us about the world? What does it tell us about how we inhabit the world, and how it inhabits us?

The idea that expression is a form of description, a form of truth, implies an investigation of the epistemic value of tone, gesture, mood, feeling, qualitative particularity—everything that surrounds and permeates the content of signification and representation without actually being that content. This dimension of experience has generally been talked about in inverse proportion to its importance precisely because it is supposed to be beyond the reach of words, to be *that* which is beyond the reach of words, even when words themselves are the medium of expression. But this ineffability, which undoubtedly belongs among the immediate effects of qualitative expression, is best understood as a deferral, not an impossibility. To the extent that we can understand expression, we can speak about it, as long as we choose the right moment and find the right language.

Doing so is important not only because, as I will go on claiming, the qualitative makes key contributions to conceptual content, but also because, to take the claim a step further, it is qualitative expression that animates conceptual content. Expression is what imparts to this content, as manifest in social and material reality, the dimension of aliveness that makes reality a world and not just an environment. Hans-Georg Gadamer says that language does this, which is right enough[17]—but only if one includes the mutual address of language and the qualitative. Language as propositional and illocutionary completes the work of world-making only through language as expressive, a source of constructive description and ambient feeling, a medium of the music of knowledge.

Music as art assumes an exemplary role in this project because its meaning is capable of expressive, qualitative articulation in the absence of indicative content (concepts, reference, illocutionary force), or independent of it (the case of songs, illustrative music, and program music). This capacity has given music its historical role as the beyond-significance, and in particular its synonymy with whatever lies beyond the reach of words. But of course music has a deep elective affinity for words, as its most prevalent form, song, clearly declares, just as words, well used, embody a music that is at least as much literal as figurative, involving tone, pace, accent, attack, breath, timbre, and so on. The secrets of expression are the secrets of music, which I have been—here and elsewhere—at pains both to uncover and to leave in place.

This is not to say, as was claimed traditionally, that music lacks semantic value, nor, following Nancy, that semantic value induces a lack in music. It *is* to say that the medium of music's semantic value is precisely its expressive and qualitative articulation. This articulation simultaneously embodies and defers the semantic value of musical expression. Nancy notwithstanding, the apparent muteness of this embodiment is not an end term. It is a question, the question of the relationship between expression and truth. And this is a question that (as I've often proposed) music raises in primary, paradigmatic form. In our real-world reactions to music we act as if the truth of expression were at stake, but our thinking about music has lagged behind and a sense of music's role in culture has lagged along with it.

It is past time to change the language game. Music has, as *Musical Meaning* demonstrates, an a priori ambiguity that defines it. Its expressiveness can be referred to its contingent historical and cultural circumstances or to its independent sounding presence; what it expresses is particularized in the first case and universalized in the second. There is a continuous movement between these possibilities whereby the music sidesteps any particular meanings to express its own musicality (a valued quality that does, however, assume different identities at different times, from cosmic harmony to the artwork in and for itself), while at the same time it fosters a plenitude of semantic applications by the way it particularizes its expressiveness.

To adapt the language of Deleuze and Guattari, what we hear in music is the becoming-tone of meaning and the becoming-meaning of tone. (This formation, the syncategorematic *becoming-*, designates a state of constant, unfinished, unfinishable transition between two ideal conditions, neither of which ever appears wholly as such.)[18] That's why, despite the proverbial inability to give verbal form to what music expresses, all musical culture is incessantly talky. The talk betokens a desire to trust expression as a kind of truth even if we can't say just why we should or what kind of truth this is. But it turns out that the very music that used to provoke these hesitations is the best means of overcoming them. Once you rub the glass a little, music is a hermeneutic window into expression and truth.

Listening at that window suggests two cardinal theses.

First, expression is the dynamic element that imparts descriptive realism to the indicative (signifying and representational) content of cultural products.

It does so because, as Wittgenstein suggests, expression is performative. It constitutes experience in being experienced. It exists in a series of repetitions in both space and time, but this fact does not entail a nominalist view (like Judith Butler's) that would reduce it to such a series. On the contrary, part of the experience created is precisely the experience of what might be called everyday or relative transcendence, the palpable but unreified reality of what might seem like an abstraction or a fiction. The expressive reality is not a chimera created by such repetitions; it is the disposition that makes participation in the series of repetitions possible and meaningful, or, if you will, it just *is* those repetitions under the auspices of their possibility and meaningfulness.

What expression creates is a phenomenal reality that is only intermittently dependent on material reality. It is a reality that, like music, can be summoned up at will from its absence, and that assures its own continuity by its protean capacity to assume new and different meanings (uses, applications, pertinences, connections) with each repetition. This is a reality that exceeds material reality without necessitating ideas of absolute transcendence or ethereality. For those (like me) who don't regard such ideas as truths, expression remains their essential medium. For those (like me) who regard the same ideas as myths or metaphors, expression is even more essential because it is the means by which the world becomes meaningful in the absence of higher meaning. Relative transcendence becomes the partner of an immanence it does not oppose. The worldly space thus continuously created between what amounts to spirit and matter is the essential sphere of human conduct. Expression is the lingua franca there.

Second, to understand expression is (therefore) to understand the reality conditions that the descriptive realism of cultural products creates for itself. An expression constitutes a description of the reality it creates; to understand the one makes it possible to understand the other. The medium of this understanding is interpretation, an unreeling of language as a kind of higher-order expression enclosing and extending expression itself. The task of interpretation in this sense—and of course, it can always go wrong—is to specify and amplify the descriptive realism of the initial expression.

Like Wittgenstein's, this view of expression departs from the informal metaphysics, the spontaneous philosophy, of traditional accounts. These fall loosely into two familiar groups, one psychological, the other semiotic, both of which separate expressive actions from the "feelings" (here an omnibus term) that the actions express. Psychological models suggest that expression originates in a feeling within one person who transmits it to, arouses it in, another or others. Semiotic models suggest that expressions signify or symbolize feelings without requiring their presence in either sender or receiver. Perhaps neither of these models is entirely avoidable, but both of them subordinate expression to the authority of prior states and therefore fail to account for its constructive, creative, performative power.

Wittgenstein gets closer to that power by showing that the feeling expressed is indistinguishable from the act or utterance of expression. Expression just is that indistinction in the positive form of an event. We do not have to identify it further. But this model does have a blind spot, which lodges in the assumption that expressive acts subsume or, better, consume their expressive content. By this account the force of expression does not extend beyond the borders of the act and its occasion. But what is there to stop it? Doesn't the necessity of reply immediately open the possibilities of recalling, recounting, repeating, retelling, remaking? We can never be sure when or if an expression is finished. Its borders, if it has them, are not fixed. I may be shaken or uplifted by an expressive act that has a long aftermath in both my spoken and unspoken experience. The substance of the expression in this case extends far beyond the act, eventually almost discarding the act as one was supposed to discard Wittgenstein's famous ladder ("Whoever understands me . . . must, so to speak, throw away the ladder [of my propositions] after he has climbed it"[19]). Schumann's treatment of the theme "Wie aus der Ferne" is virtually an allegory of this persistence and its vicissitudes, which Wittgenstein oddly suspends by confining himself to the "tune" rather than what happens to it. On the other hand, I may disregard an expressive act as soon as it's done; I may scarcely notice that the act does not become complete, has not become complete, until I have done something in partaking of it. But even then I cannot absolutely be sure of being done with it. Every expressive act occurs at a crossroads. What actually happens is less important than the irreducible openness of the question of what may happen, may always happen, may always have happened, may always be what will have happened.

That openness, which coincides with the necessary mutuality of the expressive act and the reply that reexpresses it, marks the point of theoretical sufficiency. It looms just beyond the border that Wittgenstein finds but does not cross. To reach the open one has to proceed in the spirit of his investigations but against their letter. One must, that is, not sidestep or nullify but replace the metaphysics of mind. Nowadays cognitive science and neuropsychology seem poised to claim the role long since vacated by the Cartesian ghost in the machine, but for the purposes of understanding expression, of taking expression seriously, they so far have had little to offer. The metaphysics has to be replaced, not by a science of mind, but by a new sort of phenomenology more attuned to the media of expression than to a model of consciousness. In this phenomenology of expression, bracketing the phenomenon is a license for relative transcendence, and constructive description is the instrument of a conditional realism.

To think in this mode may demand that our thinking sometimes take the form of a kind of prose poetry. As I said in the preface, we need not only to think about expression but also to think with it. In the writings of a Wittgenstein, a Derrida, a Nietzsche, that is exactly the way thinking works already. The mentality that would dismiss the results as fabulation (perhaps even by "appreciating" them) is caught helplessly by an allegiance to either dogmatic belief or hard-core empiricism—opposite systems that agree on what they don't like. Such systems represent the kind of trap invoked by Wittgenstein when he said, famously, that his aim was to show the fly the way out of the fly bottle (*PI*, 103). The bottle is hard to escape, partly because it may go unrecognized or be disavowed by the fly, and partly because the only language capable of answering the fly's objections is the language the fly objects to. I don't know that it is possible to argue anyone into or out of a worldview that seems foundational. But it may be possible to make another worldview attractive enough to draw new visitors. Some of them may even decide to move there.

Expression is acoustic at its origin; the acoustic is expressive at its origin. We need to consider that its numinous particles are not just any phenomena but *acoustic* phenomena. And that in turn requires a return to the onto-phenomenology of the auditory and in particular the difference between hearing and listening broached earlier in this chapter. Hearing begins with but *is* not an involuntary sensory registration. Hearing is the recording of an aspect. Listening begins with but *is* not a giving of attention. Listening is an act, and not just a corporeal act: It is an expressive/illocutionary act, and moreover the precondition for receiving other such acts as addressed to the subject—that is, for hearing.

Listening appropriates hearing so that hearing approximates listening—or rather a-proximates it: We will come to that. Listening is a kind of utterance by which utterance is received. It is a performance composed partly as something done, partly as something done with or to, partly as a gift, partly as a meeting. Listening is hearing-as, or better, it *becomes* hearing-as. And the "-as" is often the most elusive of numinous particles. As you can hear, if you've been listening, hearing is easy; listening is hard.

What, then, happens when we listen? And in particular when we listen to music, which is the exceptional condition of listening that, precisely as such, defines what it means to listen? When and how, in music, does listening become reflective? social? historical? ontological? hermeneutic? aesthetic?

The answer, in a series that begins with "reflective," is: Listening remarks (on) itself when it gives what it hears the form of a "haunting melody." The term comes from Theodor Reik, a member of the Freud circle who wrote about being obsessed after the death of a colleague by the auditory memory of a theme from Mahler's Second Symphony.[20] Oliver Sacks recently suggested calling such maddeningly persistent musical memories "brainworms": no romance of being "haunted" for him.[21] Both Sacks, a neurologist, and Reik, a psychoanalyst, think of this music "stuck in the head" as aberrant, linked in some way to pathology. Yet both also acknowledge a link to normality, or rather to the very foundations of the sense of normality. Sacks connects the persistence of the brainworm to our desire for the repetition of what gives pleasure; the adult brain finds in the melody a relic of the child's insistence on hearing the same story, the same words, *again*. Reik thinks of the expressive quality of the melody as a residue of conflict, trauma, or intense emotion— something the self isn't finished with. For Sacks, the brainworm exaggerates the sense of well-being with which we would like to identify ourselves; for Reik, the haunting melody returns us to a critical moment in our emotional lives, a moment that we may keep secret even from ourselves but that is one of the keys to who we are.

I would like to retain Reik's emphasis on the secret while setting aside his assumption of obsession (no brainworms for me). The result is the kind of melody that Schumann wrote and Wittgenstein heard "wie aus der Ferne": a musical utterance that bears in advance the trace of its own recurrence. The haunting melody in this sense recurs as something familiar that becomes unknown in being heard. Its effect is the reverse of the uncanny, which in its classical Freudian formulation appears as something unknown but all too familiar.[32] The haunting melody does not come to mind as a quotation or citation. It comes as something already heard but not yet, perhaps never yet, heard-as. For Nancy, the value of listening lies in suspending (ideally forever) the moment in which hearing-as returns us to the known in a new form.

The return is always a loss; suspending it is an opportunity to identify with the music as extended and thus unfathomable subjectivity. But restoring the arc between listening and an *-as* does not deny the extension, the singular self-pluralization of the self that Nancy calls for. Listening as reply, listening through the haunting melody to the auditory lighting up of an aspect, does not disenchant or petrify. On the contrary: It realizes the dissemination of self in musical form, as (that "as" again) a polyphony of answering acts.

That is what we find in Wittgenstein, for whom the question of reflective listening led back to "Wie aus der Ferne," heard not only as a haunting melody but as the very model of haunting melody, a melody haunting in advance of anyone's listening. To be haunted by this melody is not only to hear it recur as the expression of pastness. To be haunted by it is also to hear the melody as coming from the distance to *become* the distance in search of an *-as* to measure it. That is how the music (or its recording, the mechanical mode of haunting melody) becomes the most "elaborate and exact" expression of "long, long ago" that Wittgenstein can imagine.

Music like this, music about listening, is relatively rare because it is a self-conscious disclosure of the condition of possibility for listening unselfconsciously. What is that condition?

The answer lies in the peculiar character of listening to music, which sets it apart from listening to ambient sound or to speech. Suppose that Heidegger is right that language, as such, "speaks" by making things present despite their material absence. Language brings the distant near but also brings the distance near, and so brings you into proximity to the distance, brings the distance to you.[23] Music does the opposite: It brings you into the distance, brings you to the distance. The feel of this transit (or transfer, transference, transport) is the feel of speech reversed: Instead of nearing you with the resonance of an absent object, music makes your presence resonate through the distance of the object's absence. But not always.

Music does this until it becomes too loud, at which point there is a sudden recoil and distance is abolished. The loud sound comes like a blow and startles even when one expects it. This recoil is basic to the onto-phenomenology of music (onto-phenomenology: that shape of experience in which appearance is what there is, in which being is appearing-as, being-as. This is not a matter of the immateriality of appearance but, rather, precisely its materiality where what appears is framed as an occasion for musing—contemplation and speculation). Much of musical aesthetics turns on this oddity. With music there is transport to the distance—or no distance. Intimate distance, of the kind basic to the onto-phenomenology of speech, is withheld, and often presented in the act of its withholding. ("Wie aus der Ferne" does that, its theme never dropping the veils of the pulsation, the syncope, that enwraps it.) Much of the intensity of our response to music stems from the desire to make what is distanced more intimate, a desire that music often awakens but rarely fulfils. Music when we listen to it places us in a condition of what I will call a-proximation, playing on the paradox of the approximate, which combines non-proximity with near-proximity because, after all, near-proximity *is* non-proximity. But not always.

Happily, not always. Music in the state of haunting melody *can* place itself and the listening to it in the exceptional state of intimate distance. ("Wie aus der Ferne" does that too, not in its "own" place but at the sites in the last number when the theme, already haunting before and even more haunting now, returns as a husk, in truth aus *weiter* Ferne, to surrender the sense of pastness.) But this state cannot be predetermined by any music, though it can be envisioned there. The production of intimate distance is always dependent on performance, on the event, which is to say it is dependent on the expressive power of the performative act, which is to say in turn that it is dependent on the possibility of the contact, always startling even at its calmest, between expression and truth. Here again we meet the formula of the reverse uncanny—something known that becomes unknown in being expressed.

So the aesthetics of music, and also its hermeneutics, is an affair of distance, no matter what else it may involve. But we still need to say more fully what this "distance" is, which with music hovers so tantalizingly between the literal and the figurative, the corporeal and the symbolic. The distance at issue here is not a cultural trope like, say, a Romantic horn call, but a perceptual trope: still contingent and historical but of higher generality, more like (and there is nothing more than this "like," though also nothing less) an immanent universal.

Of distance in this sense we can say that it is the condition of possibility of communication. Messages cross distance, both in time and space, but to grasp the significance of this otherwise obvious fact we need to reverse it: Distance is that gap which messages cross. Without the intent to signal, there is no (sense of) distance. All communication technologies in a sense invent the distances they bridge. And music, which, among many other things, *is* a communications technology, invents the distance of expression, which is also the distance between the is and the –*as*. Music is both the voice of this distance and its rhythm. It is the cultural form in which the music of knowledge assumes cognitive force. Or better, since music not only moves through distance and moves us into the distance and sometimes brings us into a-proximation, music is "ecstatic" in the sense of a carrying out of place, a sense that carries over into the broader sense of being "carried away." At least music may become that, from time to time, when it is listened to and not merely heard. (That is one reason why "classical" music was, and is, culturally important: because of its demand for listening. But yes, any music can carry us like a tune.) Music listened to is the ecstasy of distance.

Or at least live music is. Sound recording has its own logic of distance, which is bound up on one side with history and on the other with invisibility. Recorded sound is fully present but it always comes to us from the past. It is no accident that Wittgenstein found the fullest expression of a sense of pastness not in a live performance of "Wie aus der Ferne" but in a phonograph of one: The phonograph is a part of the distance, an instrument of distancing. Audio recording makes all music acousmatic, Wagner's invisible orchestra with a vengeance. It is never an actual transmission of an original sound but only a reproduction of it, an approximation, often a fabrication of the recording studio. Even video recording retains the traces of the technological problem of synchronizing sight and sound. Even when we listen via headphones or earbuds, the sound is *in* but not *of* the body; it is an inserted object, not a productive resonance. Distance always intrudes itself, intrudes itself everywhere.

Without distance there is no music. Speech may be heard in whispers; music not. Music is distance heard as expression. That is the truth of music and the instrument of music's relationship to truth.

Since the Enlightenment we have tended to think of expression as a symbolic act that makes the internal external, or, more precisely, that registers externally a feeling, attitude, sensation, or state of mind internal to the subject. This remains the everyday sense of the term and it persists in critical use as well. The conception goes along with the discovery, which was also the invention, of the aesthetic, and with the theories of art as production or projection, not reproduction or imitation—in M. H. Abram's classic formulation, art not as mirror but as lamp—that the aesthetic brought with it.[24]

But this concept of expression as retrieval, the taking of something out of the cabinet of self, is genealogically a transference from an older usage focused not so much on expression as on the inexpressible, largely from within the traditions of negative theology and Christian mysticism.[25] In these traditions expression is indistinguishable from description, which belongs to nature and not to spirit; the gap between the two spheres is unbridgeable. The post-Enlightenment model is a secular adaptation. The indescribable (inexpressible) divine versus the describable (expressible) natural becomes the indescribable (internal) subjective versus the describable (external) objective. Expression now separates from description and assumes the form of making the internal external, accomplishing in displaced form the previously impossible bridging of separate spheres. What is expressed remains indescribable but we can nonetheless grasp its import.

Like all such historical formations, this one cannot be undone entirely as long as it remains in cultural memory. But it can be superseded, or rendered only a moment in a more inclusive model, which is what is happening now for both technological and conceptual reasons. What higher-order model would best subsume and redescribe, that is, reexpress, the activity of expression? What *else* happens when, as a local effect of the post-Enlightenment era, expression makes the internal external? What more general process would this shift in location exemplify?

To make the internal external is to make the unapparent appear, or, in Wittgenstein's terms, to change the aspect of what comes before us. To do so is not the same as to disclose or unconceal; what expression expresses is not the hidden but the unobserved, or better perhaps, the unremarked. (The expressive does not correspond exactly to either the model of truth as disclosure or the model of truth as correspondence. Instead it preserves fragmentary elements of both: the change of perception from the former and the conjunction of terms from the latter.) In other words still, expression alters what is describable (or not) in the circumstances it addresses. The difference between expression and description is itself a matter of the aspect an utterance assumes for us. What we call a description is always the answer to an implicit question—what is that like? What we call expression puts the answer *before* the question and therefore puts the question differently when it puts the question at all.

Expression is neither personal nor private; it does not maintain the distinctions between inner and outer, obscure and clear, that it is so often thought to serve. On the contrary: Expression takes the impossibility of such distinctions as its own condition of possibility.

One distinction that expression *does* maintain is the one between the auditory and the visual. As I have stressed more than once, expression is originarily auditory. Its visual dimensions, notably gesture and posture, are primarily supplemental; even its facial form is closely linked to speech and vocalization. Expression is obviously not confined to the auditory, and the imagetext certainly mimics it in a plethora of ways, but it would be fair to say that expression incessantly *returns* to the auditory. That is one reason for its historical kinship with the evolution of hearkening. Its most iconic and pervasive element, tone, is basic to all description and in some circumstances can carry descriptive force without the help of words. The unease sometimes felt in the silence of images suggests a kernel of injury in the default of the auditory. The problem of that silence (attested to by early observers of film) may be one reason why the union of sound and the moving image was so important historically.

The best example of expression, therefore, the paradigm, is not discourse but utterance, not words per se but the vibratory substance of their intelligibility. We are back at speaking melody; we are back at melodic speech; we are back (we will never stop coming back) to saying that the question of expression is fundamentally a musical question. Gesture and posture want sound; facial expression wants speech; utterance wants utterance in reply. In brief: Ontology needs sonority. Or briefer still: Being resonates.

Resonates all around: echoes, doubles, proliferates. Expression is as much a medium as it is an action. Its affinity with sound splits the imagetext into the mute and the vocal, and sculpts the acoustic envelope of everyday communication. Expression is the tone of my utterance and also my utterance itself; it is the way I play the melody and also the melody itself. This apparent duality is not actually dual, but recursive. Expression twins itself. The tone imparts a certain concern to the utterance (but one that already belongs to the utterance) and/as the utterance imparts a certain concern to its occasion (but one that already belongs to the occasion). Expression is the music of meaning, meaning in its musical form. It is both the substance of the aesthetically extraordinary and the conduit of the uncanniness of the ordinary.

Expression is what keeps things interesting.

   —The old door sags on its hinges.
A nudge of wind and it creaks likes centuries of crows.
This is not a metaphor.
Not once it was said.

EXAMPLE 5.3 Frédéric Chopin, Prelude in C Minor, Op. 28. No. 20 (complete)

"A reflective Chopin" (nachdenklichen Chopin). Chopin's Prelude in C minor (see Example 5.3) reflects itself in a shard of broken mirror. For its first eight (of thirteen) measures, it seems like an anticipation of Wittgenstein's dream of writing a melody—just one—that would sum up a life. The eight measures form a miniature funeral march, the melody tolling in the right hand over octaves tolling in the left. The first half rises from *fortissimo;* the second half answers *piano.* And there it might have ended, and there it did end in various album copies that Chopin made of the piece. But the autograph score does not stop there. The autograph reflects, and as it reflects it breaks the symmetry of the music, and it does so not once but twice. (Many published editions, starting with the first, get this wrong, but they too do not stop after eight measures.[26]) Measures 9 through 12 repeat the second half, now *pianissimo* through the second beat of measure 10, after which a crescendo begins. How loud this crescendo should grow is uncertain, but

whatever the answer may be, the last measure, the odd one, number thirteen, cancels the rise, reverses it, further fracturing symmetry with a single chord, a detached sonority set under a fermata and marked with a descending hairpin: a fadeout. The prelude collapses into its own reflectiveness.

When I hear Chopin's Prelude in C minor, the music slips away from my ears, though it doesn't move. The crescendo at the close always seems too loud, no matter how small it is, as if the music were trying (even at the cost of self-deception) to regain a presence it had already lost. The melody in the right hand wants to be there, *here*, where it cannot any longer be. All it can do is crumble into the motionless closing chord, which means too much and expresses too little.

When I play Chopin's Prelude in C minor, the music recedes under my hands, which nonetheless bring it closer. The firm feel of the left-hand octaves, descending steadily across the span of the melody, does not diminish when I try to play the *pianissimo* and does not increase when (with as much restraint as I can muster) I try to play the crescendo. The octaves literally embody my grasp of the music, but only in the second half, where (instead of rocking, as they do in the first segment) they go step by step to the end, the dark, the depths. The truth somehow lies there (take that as you will), extended by the pedal under the bland closing chord.

The left hand, then, or the right? The right brain or the left?

"Couldn't we think that a man who has never known music and who comes to us and hears someone playing a reflective Chopin, that he would be convinced that this is a language and we just want to keep the meaning secret from him?"

We will never understand the mind by understanding the brain until we understand the brain in the language of mind.

Wittgenstein's gramophone was like the piano in one respect, which is perhaps why the music in which he heard the past recaptured by a recording was piano music. To play a record, one had to set the tone arm of the machine on the edge of the disk by hand: gently, with precision. Like the piano, this gramophone demanded a touch, and a touch that in conveying itself would yield expressive sound. True expressiveness hung upon that touch, which in turn hung upon a point, a fine point, the tip of the diamond stylus that would circle the record's grooves. The melody in which a feeling, even a life, might be crystallized would arise, at a touch, from the point of a crystal.

1. Martin Heidegger, *Being and Time*, trans. John Macquarrie and Edward Robinson (Oxford: Blackwell, 1962), 198–203.

2. Quoted by Erik Heijerman, "Three Bars by Wittgenstein," trans. Hans Peterse, *Musicology* 5 (2005): 393–95.

3. See Berthold Hoeckner, "Schumann and Romantic Distance," *Journal of the American Musicological Society* 50 (1997), 91–109.

4. Ian Hacking, *Rewriting the Soul: Multiple Personality and the Sciences of Memory* (Princeton: Princeton University Press, 1995), 23–24.

5. Stanley Cavell, "The Argument of the Ordinary," in *Conditions Handsome and Unhandsome: The Constitution of Emersonian Perfectionism* (Chicago: University of Chicago Press, 1988), 64–100. In a densely technical argument with Saul Kripke over rules and criteria in the *Philosophical Investigations*, Cavell regards "inclination" as effectively synonymous with "disposition" and suggests that Wittgenstein takes it as "an instance and emblem of the voice I have in thinking" (p. 64). But the argument of the ordinary also suggests a more colloquial alternative, especially as "I am inclined" is used in English, as Wittgenstein uses it here. In the prevalent language games involving the phrase, "I am inclined" marks something I will do, announced, depending on my inflection, politely or imperiously; or it marks in a friendly way something I will do with you after you ask me what I want to do; or it announces a threat ("I am inclined to throw the book at you"). It rarely marks hesitation or doubt without the explicit addition of a "but. . . ."

6. On constructive description, see Kramer, *Interpreting Music* (Berkeley: University of California Press, 2010), 52–66; and "Subjectivity Unbound: Music, Language, Culture," *The Cultural Study of Music*, 2nd ed., ed. Martin Clayton, Trevor Herbert, and Richard Middleton (New York: Routledge, 2011), 395–406.

7. Martin Heidegger, "Words," trans. Joan Stambaugh, in *On the Way to Language* (New York: HarperCollins, 1982), 152; Heidegger is paraphrasing, commenting on, and reaffirming the last line of a poem by Stefan George, "The Word": "No thing may be where the word breaks off" (Kein ding sei wo das wort gebricht). This line, Heidegger claims, enacts a revelation of "the be-thinging of the thing in the word" (p. 151).

8. Schumann's epigraph is one of two; the other attaches to the ninth number and refers to Florestan, the sensitive Eusebius's exuberant partner as an alter ego for Schumann. In the first edition, the different numbers are signed with the initials of one persona, the other, or both. The original text of Eusebius's epigraph reads: "Ganz zum Überfluss meinte Eusebius noch Folgendes; dabei sprach aber viel Seligkeit aus seinen Augen."

9. Jean-Luc Nancy, *Being Singular Plural*, trans. Robert D. Richardson and Anne E. O'Byrne (Stanford: Stanford University Press, 2000).

10. Jean-Luc Nancy, *Listening*, trans. Charlotte Mandell (New York: Fordham University Press, 2007), 59, subsequent citations in text; and Lacan, *The Seminar*

of Jacques Lacan, Book VII: The Ethics of Psychoanalysis, 1959–60, ed. Jacques-Alain Miller, trans. Dennis Potter (New York: Norton, 1992), 54.

11. *Listening*, 59, parentheses omitted.

12. *Listening*, 59.

13. *Listening*, 59.

14. *Listening*, 59.

15. The 1879 version of the second edition, edited by Clara Schumann, carries a problematic metronome marking of quarter note = 132, which is much too fast. As with many of the Schumanns' markings, pianists ignore it; Example 5.2 omits it. Similarly, Example 5.1 omits the marking for "Wie aus der Ferne."

16. Jacques Ranciére, "The Aesthetic Dimension: Aesthetics, Politics, Knowledge," *Critical Inquiry* 36 (2009), 16.

17. Hans-Georg Gadamer, *Truth and Method*, 2nd rev. ed., trans. Joel Weinsheimer and Donald G. Marshall (New York: Continuum, 1996), 443.

18. Gilles Deleuze and Félix Guattari, *A Thousand Plateaus: Capitalism and Schizophrenia* (1980), trans. Brian Massumi (Minneapolis: University of Minnesota Press, 1987), 232–309.

19. Wittgenstein, *Tractatus Logico-Philosophicus*, trans. D. F. Pears and B. F. McGuiness (London: Routledge and Kegan Paul, 1961), 151.

20. Theodor Reik, *The Haunting Melody: Psychoanalytic Experiences in Life and Music* (New York: Farrar, Strauss, and Young, 1953), 221–23. For a detailed account, see Philippe Lacoue-Labarthe, "Echo of the Subject" in *Typography: Mimesis, Philosophy, Politics* (1979), trans. Christopher Fynsk (Stanford: Stanford University Press, 1998), 139–207.

21. Oliver Sacks, *Musicophilia: Tales of Music and the Brain* (New York: Random House, 2007), 41–48.

22. Sigmund Freud, "The Uncanny" (1919), trans. Alix Strachey, in *Writings on Art and Literature*, ed. Neil Hertz (Stanford: Stanford University Press, 1997), 193–233, esp. 195–201, 217.

23. Heidegger, "Language," in *Poetry Language Thought*, trans. Albert Hofstadter (New York: HarperCollins, 2001), 196.

24. M. H. Abrams, *The Mirror and the Lamp: Romantic Theory and the Critical Tradition* (New York: Norton, 1953), esp. 21–26, 48–70.

25. Giorgio Agamben, *Language and Death: The Place of Negativity*, trans. Karen E. Pinkus with Michael Hardt (Minneapolis: University of Minnesota Press, 1991), 6–37.

26. On the publication history, see Thomas Higgins, *Chopin: Preludes, Op. 28, An Authoritative Score* (New York: Norton, 1973), 6–7, 68–69. For more on the significance of the C-minor Prelude's strange design, with reference to both historical circumstances and constructive description, see Kramer, "Subjectivity Unbound: Music, Language, Culture," in *The Cultural Study of Music*, ed. Martin Clayton, Trevor Herbert, and Richard Middleton, 2nd ed. (New York: Routledge, 2011), 395–406.

INDEX OF NAMES

INDEX OF CONCEPTS